RENEW International

WHY CATHOLIC?
JOURNEY THROUGH THE CATECHISM

LIFE
IN
CHRIST

Walking with God

The publisher gratefully acknowledges use of the following:
The Scripture quotations contained herein are from the New Revised Standard Version Bible (containing the Old and New Testaments with the Apocryphal/Deuterocanonical Books), copyright © 1989 by the Division of Christian Education of the National Council of the Churches of Christ in the U.S.A., and are used by permission. All rights reserved.

English translation of the *Catechism of the Catholic Church* for the United States of America Copyright © 1994, United States Conference of Catholic Bishops—Libreria Editrice Vaticana. English translation of the *Catechism of the Catholic Church: Modifications from the Editio Typica* Copyright © 1997, United States Conference of Catholic Bishops—Libreria Editrice Vaticana. Used with permission.

Excerpt from *Vatican Council II, The Basic Edition: Constitutions, Decrees, Declarations*, edited by Austin Flannery, O.P., copyright © 1996, Costello Publishing Company, Northport, NY, are used by permission of the publisher, all rights reserved. No part of this excerpt may be reproduced, stored in a retrieval system, or transmitted in any form or by any means—electronic, mechanical, photocopying, recording or otherwise, without express permission of Costello Publishing Company.

NIHIL OBSTAT
Reverend Lawrence E. Frizzell, D.Phil.
Archdiocese of Newark Theological Commission
Censor Librorum

IMPRIMATUR
Most Reverend John J. Myers, J.C.D., D.D.
Archbishop of Newark

Cover design by James F. Brisson

Library of Congress Control Number: 2005900777

ISBN 1-930978-37-5
(Previously ISBN 1-930978-16-2)

RENEW International
1232 George Street
Plainfield, NJ 07062-1717
Phone   908-769-5400
www.renewintl.org
www.WhyCatholic.org

Printed and bound in the United States of America.

Contents

✝ ✝ ✝

Acknowledgments

✝ ✝ ✝

RENEW International gratefully acknowledges those who have contributed to this work:

Artists and their Publishers

Ansgar Holmber, CSJ, for the illustrations on pages 2, 9, 21, 23, 27, 36, 44, 48, 50, 70, 76, 77
Copyright © Living the Good News. Used by permission of the publisher.

Gerardine Mueller, OP, for the illustrations on pages 4, 11, 15, 16, 34, 42, 56, 64, 72

The illustration on page 34 quotes verse 4 of the song "Gift of Finest Wheat," by Omer Westendorf, © 1977 Archdiocese of Philadelphia. Used by permission.

Joan Smith, OP, for the illustration on page 30

Therese Denham for the illustration on page 65

Carol L. Smith, CSJ, for the illustration (from the CD "Graphics for the Liturgical Seasons") on page 29

Piloters

Small Christian community members who piloted the materials and offered helpful insights

Foreword

✝ ✝ ✝

My calling as a bishop challenges me to ever seek means to assist solid faith formation and growth in holiness. Foundational in meeting this need is the *Catechism of the Catholic Church*, which so magnificently conveys the wisdom of the Holy Spirit in guiding the Church's tradition in following Jesus Christ.

The Introduction to the U.S. bishops' document *Our Hearts Were Burning Within Us* speaks of how disciples of Jesus share in proclaiming the Good News to the entire world.

> Every disciple of the Lord Jesus shares in this mission. To do their part, adult Catholics must be mature in faith and well equipped to share the Gospel, promoting it in every family circle, in every church gathering, in every place of work, and in every public forum. They must be women and men of prayer whose faith is alive and vital, grounded in a deep commitment to the person and message of Jesus.

Why Catholic? Journey through the Catechism is well designed to enable this goal to become reality. It faithfully breaks open the contents of the *Catechism* for reflection and assimilation by individuals or participants in small faith-sharing groups. The sharing enables participants to take greater personal ownership of their faith and to move from an inherited faith to deep faith conviction.

This exploration of divinely revealed truth has a formative effect on peoples' lives. The "yes" of consent to faith emulates Mary's fiat, her "yes" to God's will. A prayerful openness to God's will is the path to holiness.

Why Catholic? seeks to be an instrument for faith formation and a call to holiness. Saints in everyday life are the strength of the Church, which is always renewing itself in fidelity to the mission of Christ and in service to the needs of our society. I heartily commend this effort in making the *Catechism of the Catholic Church* more accessible to the faithful.

Most Reverend John J. Myers, J.C.D., D.D.
Archbishop of Newark

Introduction

✝ ✝ ✝

Many Catholics have inherited the faith without knowing why they are Catholic. They have never been exposed to the solid faith formation provided by the *Catechism of the Catholic Church*. For that reason, RENEW International has taken the four parts of the *Catechism* and has developed this series, *Why Catholic? Journey through the Catechism*.

Why Catholic? is an easy-to-use tool for individuals and/or small faith-sharing communities to reference, read, pray over, and treasure the rich resources of the *Catechism of the Catholic Church*. By using these materials, we hope participants will study the *Catechism of the Catholic Church* in greater depth, internalize its teachings, share faith in Jesus Christ, learn more about their faith, and let their faith illuminate every aspect of their lives.

The reflections offer people a "taste" of the content of the *Catechism*. *Why Catholic?* is not intended to be a compendium or a total summary of the *Catechism*, but rather, a way for people to try to become more faithful to the teachings of the Church. We encourage people to read sections of the *Catechism* before, during, and after each session.

In a way, *Why Catholic?* is a guidebook to the *Catechism*. Yet it is much more. It invites readers and participants to a mature faith by nourishing and strengthening laywomen and men in their calling and identity as people of faith.

These four books may be a way for people to uncover their own story, their own journey about being Catholic. What does it mean to be Catholic? Why they stay? Why they became Catholic? To assist in discovering their story, we recommend participants keep a journal and after each session spend some time journaling key beliefs of the Catholic Church and their personal insights. What a valuable treasure they will have to meditate on and perhaps share with others.

Part One of the *Catechism of the Catholic Church* focuses on the great mysteries of our faith. In Part Two the emphasis is on celebrating our faith in sacramental liturgy. Part Three helps to explain the moral teachings of the Catholic faith. Part Four looks more deeply at our relationship with God and how we nurture that relationship in prayer.

This third book in the *Why Catholic?* Series, *Life in Christ: Walking with God* breaks open Part Three of the *Catechism*. The first part of this book centers on our freedom and responsibility, conscience, virtues, moral law, and grace. The second part concentrates on the implications of the Ten Commandments.

If you are gathering in a small community, you may wish to meet either in two six-week blocks of time or over twelve consecutive weeks to cover all the sessions. Your community may also wish to use the other three books based on the *Catechism—The Profession of Faith: What We Believe* (Part One), *The Celebration of the Christian Mystery: Sacraments* (Part Two), and *Christian Prayer: Deepening My Experience of God* (Part Four).

May these reflections lead you to a closer, more vibrant relationship with our loving God.

N.B. Throughout the *Why Catholic?* Series constant and direct reference is made to the *Catechism*. Many sentences in the **Exploring the Catechism** sections are direct quotes. To make these easily identifiable, direct quotes are in bold print. Elsewhere, what the *Catechism* says is summarized and paraphrased: this is in regular print. Whether directly quoted or paraphrased, material from the *Catechism* is identified by the paragraph number from the *Catechism* in bold print and in parentheses, that is, **(000).**

Faith-Sharing Principles and Guidelines

When we gather as Christians to share our faith and grow together in community, it is important that we adhere to certain principles. The following Theological Principles and Small Community Guidelines will keep your community focused and help you to grow in faith, hope, and love.

Principles

- God leads each person on his or her spiritual journey. This happens in the context of the Christian community.
- Christ, the Word made flesh, is the root of Christian faith. It is because of Christ, and in and through him that we come together to share our faith.
- Faith sharing refers to the shared reflections on the action of God in one's life experience as related to Scripture and the faith of the Church. Faith sharing is not discussion, problem solving, or Scripture study. The purpose is an encounter between a person in the concrete circumstances of one's life and a loving God, leading to a conversion of heart.
- The entire faith-sharing process is an expression of prayerful reflection.

Guidelines

- Constant attention to respect, honesty, and openness for each person will assist the community's growth.
- Each person shares on the level where he or she feels comfortable.
- Silence is a vital part of the total process. Participants are given time to reflect before any sharing begins, and a period of comfortable silence might occur between individual sharings.
- Persons are encouraged to wait to share a second time until others who wish to do so have contributed.
- The entire community is responsible for participating and faith sharing.
- Confidentiality is essential, allowing each person to share honestly.
- Action flowing out of the small community meetings is essential for the growth of individuals and the community.

A Note to Small Community Leaders

Small Community Leaders are...

- People who encourage participation and the sharing of our Christian faith.
- People who encourage the spiritual growth of the community and of its individual members through communal prayer, a prayerful atmosphere at meetings, and daily prayer and reflection on the Scriptures.
- People who move the community to action to be carried out between meetings. They are not satisfied with a self-centered comfort level in the community but are always urging that the faith of the community be brought to impact on their daily lives and the world around them.
- Community builders who create a climate of hospitality and trust among all participants.

Small Community Leaders are not...

- **Theologians:** The nature of the meeting is faith sharing; should a theological or scriptural question arise, the leader should turn to the pastor or staff to seek guidance.
- **Counselors:** The small communities are not intended for problem solving. This is an inappropriate setting to deal with emotionally laden issues of a personal nature. The leader is clearly not to enter the realm of treating people with emotional, in-depth feelings such as depression, anxiety, or intense anger. When someone moves in this direction, beyond faith sharing, the leader should bring the community back to faith sharing. With the help of the pastor or staff, the person should be advised to seek the assistance of professional counseling.
- **Teachers:** The leaders are not teachers. Their role is to guide the process of the faith sharing as outlined in the materials.

N.B. The *Why Catholic? Small Community Leader Guide* is designed to assist small community leaders in their crucial role in facilitating a *Why Catholic?* small community.

How to Use This Book

Whenever two or more of us gather in the name of Jesus, we are promised that Christ is in our midst (see Matthew 18:20). This book helps communities to reflect on the Scriptures and the *Catechism of the Catholic Church.* It is most helpful if some members of the group or the group as a whole have the Scriptures and the *Catechism* at their meeting.

Those who have met in small communities will be familiar with the process. In this book based on the *Catechism,* however, there is particular emphasis on celebrating our faith in sacramental liturgy. These reflections make demands upon our reflective nature and help in the formation of our Catholic values. THEREFORE, IT IS IMPORTANT THAT PARTICIPANTS CAREFULLY PREPARE FOR THE SESSION BEFORE COMING TO THE MEETING. They are encouraged to read and reflect on the session itself, the Scripture passage(s) cited, and the sections of the *Catechism of the Catholic Church,* and the pages from the *United States Catholic Catechism for Adults* referenced.

If the community has not met before or if participants do not know each other, take time for introductions and to get acquainted. People share most easily when they feel comfortable and accepted in a community.

Prayer must always be at the heart of our Christian gatherings. Following any necessary **Introductions**, sessions begin with a time of prayer—**Lifting Our Hearts.** There are suggested songs, some of which may be found in the parish worship aid. Other appropriate songs may be used. The Music Resources section (page 76) indicates where the suggested songs may be found as CDs or cassettes, in printed form, or in some cases, as downloadable mp3 files. If songs are copyright, remember you need to request permission before making copies of either the words or the music. The contact information for permissions can be found in the Music Resources section.

Each week, an action response—**Living the Good News**—is recommended. After the first week, the leader encourages participants to share how they put their faith in action by following through on their **Living the Good News** commitment from the previous session.

Following **Lifting Our Hearts,** and **Living the Good News,** there is an initial reflection on the *Catechism* entitled **Exploring the *Catechism.*** The next section, **Pondering the Word,** offers a Scripture reference that one participant proclaims aloud from the Bible. Together, the *Catechism* and Scripture selections will give the community members the opportunity to reflect on what Jesus has said and to share their faith on the particular topic. Sharing could take about 15 minutes.

Next, the small community continues **Exploring the *Catechism*** and then considers the **Sharing Our Faith** questions. Faith-sharing groups vary greatly in their background and composition. In some sessions, the group may wish to start with the question: What insights into my faith did I gain from this session? Explain. Allow approximately 25 minutes for **Sharing Our Faith,** making sure the last question is always considered.

In coming to closure, each session offers some ideas for an individual or group action—**Living the Good News.** Here, participants reflect on how God is inviting them to act during the coming week—how to bring their faith into their daily lives. The ideas presented are merely suggestions. It is important that group members choose an action that is both measurable and realistic.

Each session then concludes with **Lifting Our Hearts.**

Suggested Format of the Sharing Sessions (1½ hours)

Introductions (when the group is new or when someone joins the group)	
Lifting Our Hearts	10 minutes
Sharing the Good News	5 minutes
Exploring the *Catechism*	10 minutes
Scripture: Pondering the Word and Sharing Question	15 minutes
Exploring the *Catechism* (continued)	10 minutes
Sharing Our Faith	25 minutes
Living the Good News	10 minutes
Lifting Our Hearts	5 minutes

Sharing beyond the Group

As a group, you will be using this book as the focus for your sharing. You should consider how the fruits of your sharing can be taken beyond the confines of this group. For example, if you are parents, you could be asking what part of your faith exploration can be shared with your children. RENEW International has designed a resource, entitled *RENEWING FAMILY FAITH*, to help you achieve exactly this.

RENEWING FAMILY FAITH offers a two-page full-color bulletin for every Session contained in the *Why Catholic?* faith-sharing books. You will find a full description of this invaluable resource on pages 82-83.

Session 1
The Beatitudes

✝✝✝

Suggested environment

Bible, candle, and, if possible, the *Catechism of the Catholic Church*. *Begin with a quiet, reflective atmosphere.*

Lifting Our Hearts

Song

"Lord, We're So Precious to You," Julienne Johnson, *RENEW the Face of the Earth, Seasons 1 and 2*, White Dove Productions, Oregon Catholic Press (OCP)

Pray together

Come Holy Spirit, open our hearts as we begin our reflections together. We need your transforming action in our lives.

The leader prays each line beginning with "Sometimes...." All respond by praying the corresponding Beatitude (see Matthew 5:1-12).

Sometimes we hear, "Blessed are those who are able to amass riches and those who depend only on themselves," **but Jesus says, "Blessed are the poor in spirit."**

Sometimes we think, "Do all you can to be happy and comfortable," **but Jesus says, "Blessed are those who mourn."**

Sometimes we get the message, "The aggressive one will prosper," **but Jesus says, "Blessed are the meek."**

Sometimes we are tempted to think, "Those who are smart can get away with illegal acts," **but Jesus says, "Blessed are those who hunger and thirst for righteousness."**

Sometimes we hear,
"Happy are those who are 'inflexible' in their dealings with others,"
but Jesus says, "Blessed are the merciful."

Sometimes we think,
"Smart are they who are shrewd and take the easy way,"
but Jesus says, "Blessed are the pure in heart."

Sometimes we hear an unspoken message,
"You should not tolerate anyone who is different from you
or does not think as you do,"
but Jesus says, "Blessed are the peacemakers."

Sometimes we are tempted to say,
"Only fools speak out against injustice,"
but Jesus says,
"Blessed are those who are persecuted for righteousness' sake."

Sometimes we hear, "You are too naive, life is more complex than that,"
but Jesus says, "Blessed are you when people revile you
and persecute you and utter all kinds of evil against you falsely."

All   **Help us, Jesus, to be transformed into you, so that**
       our thinking and acting will reflect yours. Amen.

WHO IS MY
NEIGHBOR?
LUKE 10.29

Exploring the *Catechism*

We believe that God has a purpose for each of us and we want to do God's will in our lives. When Jesus says, "I am the way, and the truth, and the life" (John 14:6), he means that he is the one true connection, the mediator, between ultimate reality, which is God, and us. He tells us who he is and *who we are*—the beloved daughters and sons of God (1 John 3:1a, 2). Jesus teaches us that moral living means treating one another as brothers and sisters, namely, as members of God's own family. In God's family, it is good to remember there are no stepsisters or stepbrothers, no half-sisters or half-brothers. We are all equal. Our faith in

Christ makes us confident that we know the truth about who we are and why we exist.

Christ has given his Church the mission to teach the truth about moral living **(2050-2051)**. The faith we believe and apply by grace to our moral lives is a gift from God. As brothers and sisters in Christ, we are given the grace to respond to Christ's love in our efforts to love one another **(2050-2051)**.

We believe that we came from God's hands, and that our destiny is to share God's glory. We have faith that Christ was sent into this world to live out his own human story, teaching us by his words and example about who we are and how God wants us to live. By his humble acceptance of suffering and death as well as by his Resurrection from the dead, Jesus shows us the way. **By his Passion, Christ delivered us from Satan and from sin. He merited for us the new life in the Holy Spirit. His grace restores what sin had damaged in us (1708).**

He forgives our sins and promises us eternal life. The person who believes in Jesus Christ becomes one with him by God's grace. United with Christ, we become adopted children of his Father in heaven **(1709)**.

By the gift of his Holy Spirit dwelling within us, God lives with us and within us, reaching out to love others through our words and actions. God's powerful presence also extends beyond the Christian family, seeking to call all people to repent, to believe in the Good News, and to love one another.

We are created in the image of God because we are able to relate freely to others and form community with them, just as the three Divine Persons relate to each other and live in a loving community.

Our faith teaches us that God has given us **"a spiritual and immortal" soul** (*Gaudium et spes* 14 § 2) **(1703)**. By the light of our intellectual power of reasoning, we are capable of knowing and understanding God's creation **(1704)**. By our free will **(1730-1748)** and the grace of God, we are able to find fulfillment **"in seeking and loving what is true and good"** (*Gaudium et spes* 15 § 2) **(1704)**. God urges us to do what is good, but, from the beginning, Satan has enticed us to do what is evil. The human struggle to know what is right and to live a moral life is marred by our inclination to sin. This is the scar that our human nature bears from the wound of original sin **(1707)**.

Christ's preaching of the Beatitudes responds to our natural desire for happiness and announces that the kingdom of heaven will be restored to us in a new and wonderful way **(1716-1718)**. United with Christ, we can overcome sin and its evil results in our lives. By our forgiveness of others, we will receive mercy for ourselves. The sorrowful, the lowly, and the meek are to be satisfied and comforted by God's friendship. Those who thirst for justice and are persecuted shall become the children of God and find a great reward in heaven. The peacemakers and those who serve with pure (unselfish) love shall inherit the earth; they shall see God, and heaven will be theirs. Now we may look forward eagerly to the coming of the reign of God in all its fullness. By the power of Christ's Spirit, our moral living is to reach its fulfillment in the experience of everlasting glory **(1715, 1719).**

Jesus gave us the following powerful words in his Sermon on the Mount to offer us a blueprint for how to live our lives. It was, in fact, the blueprint for how he lived his life. In many ways, we could say that these Beatitudes contain the "directions" for how to follow Jesus most closely.

Scripture: Pondering the Word   Matthew 5:3-12

Sharing Question

- When did I, or someone I know, live out one of these Beatitudes in a concrete way?

Exploring the *Catechism* (continued)

Christian morality finds its source in **the *grace of the Holy Spirit* given to us in Christ.** The Beatitudes teach us the ways in which we should love one another and the sacraments give us the grace to do so **(1966).** The gospel says that riches are not the answer to our hearts' longing. When the rich man asked Jesus what he must do to attain everlasting life, Jesus reminded him of the Commandments. When the man assured Jesus he kept the Commandments, Jesus looked at him with love and said there was one more thing he must do. "…sell what you own, and give the money to the poor, and you will have treasure in heaven; then come, follow me" (Mark 10:17-25). From this account, we see that our attachment to money and possessions may become an obstacle to our following the Lord.

God put us in the world to know, to love, and to serve him, and so to come to paradise. Beatitude makes us "partakers of the divine nature" and of eternal life (2 Peter 1:4; cf. John 17:3) **(1721). Such beati-**

tude surpasses the understanding and powers of man. It comes from an entirely free gift of God: whence it is called supernatural, as is the grace that disposes man to enter into the divine joy (1722).

Although personal responsibility for our attitudes, words, and actions may be limited by ignorance or other factors (1735), our God-given intelligence and free will carry with them many responsibilities (1731). We are called and enabled by God's grace to make progress in our knowledge of what is good and in our habit of choosing the good and rejecting the evil of sin (1734). The Ten Commandments, the Beatitudes, and the moral teaching of the Church describe for us the path that will lead us to heaven (1724).

The Commandments confront **us with decisive moral choices.... [They] teach us that true happiness is not found in riches or well-being, in human fame or power, or in any human achievement—however beneficial it may be—such as science, technology, and art, or indeed in any creature, but in God alone, the source of every good and of all love** (1723).

(Note: Sessions 7 through 12 speak in detail on the Commandments.)

John Henry Cardinal Newman, one of the great theologians of the Church, challenges us to think about the temptations we face, temptations to "bow down before wealth." He states that many people "measure happiness by wealth; and by wealth they measure respectability.... Wealth is one idol of the day and notoriety is a second.... Notoriety, or the making of a noise in the world—it may be called 'newspaper fame'—has come to be considered a great good in itself..." (1723).

Discipleship involves calling others to share the intimate friendship of God. Our care and concern for their needs can awaken in them a wonder and a hope about commitment to Christ. The heroic lives of the saints or of holy people point the way for us, but by God's grace, every small act of kindness and generosity is a sign of God's powerful presence among us. The witness of our humble and dedicated lives invites others to become disciples of Jesus and share in his work of love.

At one time or another, we all experience the attraction of evil. We are tempted to allow wrong attitudes, words, and actions to have a place in our hearts and our lives. We are tempted not to care, to become indifferent to the needs of others, and to focus only on ourselves. We are tempted to manipulate and control people, to use them for our own economic, sexual, or social advantage. When we see ourselves in this light, we may become frustrated and disgusted because of our weakness. St. Paul says it well: "Who will rescue me from this body of death? Thanks be to God through Jesus Christ our Lord" (Romans 7:24-25).

Now it becomes easier for us to understand why our Christian faith is so important. Jesus told his followers: "If you continue in my word, you are truly my disciples; and you will know the truth, and the truth will make you free" (John 8:31-32). Sinners that we are, we have put our faith in the Lord through his Church—the community of those who believe in him. Apart from the grace that comes to us through Christ, it would be impossible for us to know the truth about our lives. We Christians understand *who we are* only because of our faith in the divine/human story revealed to us in the Bible and taught to us by the Church. The Beatitudes help us to know who we are and how we are called to love as disciples of Christ.

Sharing Our Faith

- Perhaps our greatest challenge today as Christians is to live out gospel values. We are daily confronted with conspicuous consumerism, notoriety, and other false values. What are some cultural values that I see as being at odds with the gospel? How has my personal life been affected by these cultural values?
- When have I seen a small act of kindness or generosity as a sign of God's presence among us?
- In what ways can I or we, as an individual or as a group, respond with the values of the Beatitudes in a specific area of my or our life?

Living the Good News

Determine a specific action (individual or group) that flows from your sharing. This should be your primary consideration.

When choosing an individual action, determine what you will do and share it with the group. When choosing a group action, determine who will take responsibility for different aspects of the action.

The following are secondary suggestions:

- Be a blessing to someone this week by going out of your way to be thoughtful and kind.
- Read the Gospel of Mark, the earliest and shortest gospel, this week. Determine how you can be more like Jesus.
- Choose a specific Beatitude that you will work on in the coming month. Keep a journal and record how you do.
- Speak out more forthrightly about a cultural value that is at odds with the gospel.

As my response to the gospel of Jesus, this week I commit to _____

_____ .

Lifting Our Hearts

Pray together

O Holy Spirit,
teach us and enable us
to give witness to a culture
that has forgotten
you have called us to be a God-centered people.

Give us the grace
to move from consumerism to simplicity;
from individualism to concern for others;
from materialism
to an appreciation of the spiritual and contemplative.

Transform our desires for wealth and power
into those qualities
that will bring us
to your peace
and deepen your life in us.
We ask this through Jesus Christ our Lord. Amen.

To conclude, offer each other a sign of God's peace.

Looking Ahead

- Prepare for your next session by prayerfully reading and studying:
  - **Session 2, Freedom and Responsibility of Human Acts**;
  - Scripture: Exodus 19:3-6 and 20:1-17 (God gives the Ten Commandments); John 13:31-35, 14:15-17, 15:1-27 (the new law of love)
  - pages 310-313 on the "Fundamental Elements of Christian morality" from Chapter 23 "Life in Christ—Part I" of the *United States Catholic Catechism for Adults*

- You may like to consult the relevant paragraphs from the *Catechism of the Catholic Church*:
  - paragraphs 1730-1748 on human freedom
  - paragraphs 1749-1761 on the morality of human acts
  - paragraphs 1762-1775 on the morality of the passions

- Remember to use RENEWING FAMILY FAITH (see pages 82-83) and its helpful suggestions on how to extend the fruits of your sharing beyond your group, especially to your families.

Session 2

Freedom and Responsibility of Human Acts

✝✝✝

Suggested environment

Bible, candle, and, if possible, the *Catechism of the Catholic Church*
Begin with a quiet, reflective atmosphere.

Lifting Our Hearts

Song

"I Give My Life," Norma Wedewer and Michael Semana, *RENEW the Face of the Earth*, Seasons 3 and 4

Pray together

God our Father,
you have called us to act with justice.
You have called us to love tenderly.
You have called us to walk humbly
with you (Micah 6:8).
Teach us the power of your ways.
Help us to act justly
in all our interactions and relationships with people.
Teach us how to be in right relationship with ourselves,
with one another,
and with all of creation.
We ask for your help,
through Jesus Christ our Lord,
and in the power of the Holy Spirit. Amen.

Sharing Our Good News

*Share how you did with your **Living the Good News** from the previous session.*

Exploring the *Catechism*

As human beings, we cherish freedom. Yet with freedom comes responsibility. The *Catechism* emphasizes the freedom and responsibility that God gives us **(1730)**. We are made in God's image and likeness, free persons, able to choose between good and evil. We recognize that our freely chosen attitudes, words, and actions have consequences in our own lives and in the lives of those around us. Because we accept responsibility for what we say and do in our personal and social relationships, our freedom becomes the basis of praise or blame. Freedom and responsibility always go together.

Freedom characterizes properly human acts. It makes the human being responsible for acts of which he is the voluntary agent. His deliberate acts properly belong to him (1745).

Our freedom is not absolute. Many factors, such as psychological or cultural conditions, may adversely affect it. Force, ignorance, and fear are commonly recognized as circumstances that diminish people's responsibility for what they say or do **(1746)**.

What makes an action good or evil? The goodness or evil of an attitude, word, or action rests on three factors: the moral quality of the action itself, the intention or goal of the person who is making the moral choice, and the internal and external circumstances surrounding the action **(1750-1754)**.

Although the context or situation in which we choose good or evil may increase or diminish our praise or blame, neither praise nor blame can change the moral quality of actions that are good or evil in themselves **(1754)**. Some acts are always seriously wrong, for example: rape, child abuse, adultery, or murder. No matter how well intentioned they may be, evil actions are never justified in order to achieve good results **(1756)**. The end does not justify the means.

Our human feelings and emotions are very important aspects of our personal identities and are often the energy that drives us toward good or evil. Such passions are neither good nor evil in themselves: they may urge us toward vice or toward virtue and may become good or evil according to the decisions we make to choose good or evil goals **(1767)**.

It would be impossible for human beings to live in society without a moral code. Ethical principles and rules help us set limits, for example, to refrain from over-consumption of material things or from inappropriate sexual behavior. Moral living protects us from passions and ambitions, which are inherently insatiable. A world without limits is a world of chaos and misery. We need personal and social morality translated into ethical laws in order to live together in peace.

As you listen to the following Scripture passages, focus on the word or phrase that speaks to your heart.

Scripture: Pondering the Word   Exodus 20:1-17

Sharing Question

- The commandments are divided into two parts. The first three deal with our relationship with God, the following seven talk about our relationship with others. How do the commandments allow me to live in harmony with others?

Exploring the *Catechism* (continued)

The very first book of the Bible tells us that we are made in the image of God. This means we are *personal* beings—capable of making free decisions—accepting moral responsibility, and we are called to a relationship with God and neighbor. Genesis says that our human nature is not of our own making, but is God's creation. In the same way, we believe Christian ethics involve moral truths that are not of our own making, but come from God. We can discover these truths by our human experience, but they are also clarified and strengthened by God's revelation **(1960).** Our ethical tradition has its roots in our human nature, in the Bible, and especially in the teachings of Christ.

Christians rejoice that we may "invent" ourselves in the area of personal style. Yet, we know that we do not create ourselves in terms of our nature as human beings. God has given us rules for living, writing these in our hearts, giving us the Commandments, and instructing us gradually, as our minds and hearts grow more sensitive to the work of the Holy Spirit in the Church. There was a time, for example, when the Christian community was less aware of the evil of slavery or capital punishment. As we became more conscious of the sanctity of human freedom and human life, we changed our perceptions. We seek to live God's ways rather than our own.

Those who call themselves unbelievers reject the existence of such God-given moral truths. They say moral values are merely human inventions that may have solved practical problems in the past. For them, moral principles may seem optional or trendy: the result of a "whatever works for you" mentality.

But if objective sources like the natural law and the Ten Commandments are discarded, morality may become strictly *relative* and "what feels right for me" becomes the only acceptable standard for making ethical decisions. In this case, ethical abuses may take many different forms. For example, in the western world, the autonomy of the individual is often viewed as the only absolute value, while the good of society, of the unborn, of the poor, or of important ecological issues may be given little or no consideration. If personal freedom becomes the only criterion used to decide right from wrong, the danger of absolutism arises: whoever has the power will be the one who makes the rules. In this case, there would then be no high court of appeal beyond the beliefs of a powerful individual, the policies of a particular government, or the will of a majority.

Moreover, Christ has commissioned the Church to speak with his authority (Matthew 28:20). While the Lord has entrusted a prophetic role to the entire Christian community, he specifically gave authority to the apostles and to the pope and bishops as their successors. The Church has the responsibility to give solid direction about moral issues **(2048-2051).** Jesus brings God, the individual, and the community together when he says: "…[J]ust as you did it to one of the least of these who are members of my family, you did it to me" (Matthew 25:40).

The law of God that is written in our hearts calls us to overcome our self-centeredness. Moreover, Christ enables us, through his grace, to turn away from our tendency to use others merely as a means of fulfilling our own needs. Moral conversion involves rejecting such manipulation in

order to love God and others freely. Enabled by grace, we can grow out of our self-centeredness to become other-centered. We can follow Christ's example of unconditional caring, sincere giving, and selfless loving.

Our love grows stronger or weaker as we live our lives. In terms of our feelings, we have periods of closeness and alienation. Sometimes we feel good about ourselves, and other times we feel hopeless and futile. Our faith enables us to rise above such feelings and to interpret our experience with the wisdom that comes from God. We learn "to prize the things that are of value" and grow in our understanding of what is important. In order to live a life that has meaning and purpose beyond the merely superficial, in order to have intimate relationships that are vital to our happiness, in order to live a life that is truly human, each of us, by our faith, hope, and love, must have some contact with the invisible reality St. John describes when he says: "...God is love" (1 John 4:8).

Sharing Our Faith

- Whom do I love? What does love demand of me in these relationships?
- Whom do I not love? What does love demand of me in these relationships?
- In what areas of my life am I most grateful for the guidance given by the Church?
- When have I tried to escape my moral responsibility toward others or myself? What can I do to be more responsible?

Living the Good News

Determine a specific action (individual or group) that flows from your sharing. This should be your primary consideration.

When choosing an individual action, determine what you will do and share it with the group. When choosing a group action, determine who will take responsibility for different aspects of the action.

The following are secondary suggestions:

- Forgive a family member, a friend, or a difficult person who has hurt your feelings. Contact him or her and express your forgiveness.
- Be kind and show interest in a person you feel inclined to punish with coldness or a show of indifference.
- Pray with St. John's words, "God is love," this week. Be aware and pray for person(s) or situation(s) God brings to your attention.
- Organize a letter-writing campaign in your parish around a particular moral issue, for example, abortion, euthanasia, hunger, racism, etc. Include your mayor, governor, senator, and representative among those to whom you write.

As my response to the gospel of Jesus, this week I commit to _____

_____ .

Lifting Our Hearts

Leader: Let us pray that the Spirit of God will inspire and encourage us to know and to accomplish the work of the Lord Jesus in our daily lives.

All respond after each petition: Lord, hear our prayer.

> For the grace to respect others' freedom, we pray...*R.*
>
> For the grace to become less self-centered and more concerned with the needs of others, we pray...*R.*
>
> For the grace to love wisely and well
> the persons you have put into our lives, we pray...*R.*

Add your own intentions.

To conclude, pray the Our Father.

Looking Ahead

- Prepare for your next session by prayerfully reading and studying
  - **Session 3: Conscience**
  - Scripture: Romans 2:12-16 ("The demands of the law are written on their hearts")
  - pages 314-315 on the "Formation of Conscience" from Chapter 23 "Life in Christ—Part I" of the *United States Catholic Catechism for Adults*

- You may like to consult the relevant paragraphs from the *Catechism of the Catholic Church*:
  - paragraphs 1776-1802 on moral conscience

- Remember to use RENEWING FAMILY FAITH (see pages 82-83) and its helpful suggestions on how to extend the fruits of your sharing beyond your group, especially to your families.

Session 3
Conscience

✝✝✝

Suggested environment

Bible, candle, and, if possible, the *Catechism of the Catholic Church*
Begin with a quiet, reflective atmosphere.

Lifting Our Hearts

Song

"Yes, Lord," Tony Galla, *RENEW the Face of the Earth*,
Seasons 1 and 2

Pray together

Lord Jesus Christ, you loved your apostles and
revealed your glory to them.
As we gather together in this place,
look upon us with patience and mercy.
Grant us the grace to know
what is right and
to do what is just.
Help us walk in the way of your commandments and
to love you in all things and
above all things. Amen.

Sharing Our Good News

*Share how you did with your **Living the Good News** from the previous session.*

Exploring the *Catechism*

When we come to know people and feel comfortable with them, it is actually their moral qualities that enable us to entrust ourselves without undue fear. People who are mentally and morally sound have basically healthy and caring attitudes toward others. Our hearts often are sponta- neously touched to help people in need. At times, even perfect strangers may become the occasion for generous impulses on our part.

The Church teaches that it is our moral conscience that enjoins us to love one another, to say and do what is good, and to reject what is evil **(1777)**. Since we may not live in a Christian culture, we may need to look at norms different from those offered by our culture. **The education** and formation **of the conscience is a lifelong task.** The kind of education we need is one that teaches virtues and helps to cure **fear, selfishness and pride, resentment arising from guilt, and feelings of complacency.** We need an education for our consciences that will guarantee **freedom** and engender **peace of heart (1784).** It is often difficult for us to form our consciences because our lives have become so busy and frantic that we don't always take enough time for prayer and reflection. It is essential that we be present to ourselves in order to hear the voice of God and the voice of our consciences **(1779)**.

Conscience is the basic experience we have of ourselves choosing right from wrong, good from evil. It involves a fundamental sense of our own value and our own personal responsibility. We make a judgment that a proposed action is good or bad, and then we decide to act in a particular way. The Church says that an informed conscience must be obeyed, except in cases in which the person intends to harm himself or herself or others. The Church insists that no one should coerce or persuade another to act against his or her conscience **(1782)**.

We may very easily be ignorant of God's teachings in today's world. We can make bad judgments based on this lack of information. Each of us has an obligation to educate and form our conscience in accordance with God's law **(1785)**. We cannot hope to identify right from wrong by relying only on our own resources.

"...[I]n forming their consciences the faithful must pay careful attention to the holy and certain teaching of the church. For the Catholic Church is by the will of Christ the teacher of truth. It is its duty to proclaim and teach with authority the truth which is Christ and, at the same time, to declare and confirm by her authority the principles of the moral order which spring from human nature itself" (Vatican II, *Dignitatis humanae*, 14).

The formation of conscience involves a fundamental sense of personal responsibility for our attitudes, words, and actions. The act of conscience is to make a moral judgment that a particular attitude, word, or action is right or wrong **(1796)**. It is only in the light of the Gospel and the Church's authoritative teaching of moral truth that the Christian disciple can make prudent judgments **(1802)**. The help of the Holy Spirit will not be lacking to those who sincerely desire to follow the will of God **(1788)**.

Scripture: Pondering the Word   Romans 2:12-16

Sharing Question

- In the letter to the Romans it says: "They show that what the Law requires is written on their hearts." In what ways do I try to form my conscience so that God's law is written on my heart?

Exploring the *Catechism* (continued)

It is our conscience, our awareness of ourselves as moral beings, that makes personal relationships possible. We want to become sincere, honest, sensitive, and generous persons, not phony, deceitful, uncaring, or selfish ones. We seek to develop ethical qualities like altruism and the ability to keep confidences. We want to be lighthearted, hopeful, and loyal. We want to be insightful and honest about our own motivations, etc. It is by following the teaching and the example of Jesus Christ that we can grow in understanding and accepting the truth about our own lives and learn to love others as Christ loves us.

The key components for a good formation of conscience include quiet reflection on the Word of God, a regular examination of our lives, advice from others, and, most importantly, the teachings of the Church. We are aided in our efforts by the gifts of the Holy Spirit **(1785)**. We need to be faithful to the Scriptures, to sharing with others, to personal reflection and prayer, and to the teaching of our Church. God's transforming grace in our lives is our assurance that we are making our best effort to live true Christian lives.

Still, it is often difficult for us to

form our consciences because we are frequently distracted from reflection, self-examination, and introspection. As already stated, it is essential for us as Christians to find quiet time for ourselves in order to hear the voice of God and the voice of our consciences **(1779)**.

In order to keep the Ten Commandments and follow the Beatitudes and the moral teachings of the Church, we are challenged to form our consciences based on gospel values rather than secular ones. The world encourages us to direct our energies in the pursuit of possessions, power, popularity, and position. Jesus urges us to serve the needs of those who are hungry, thirsty, lonely, and oppressed. We are to hunger and thirst for justice, to comfort all God's people, and to find rest from our labors by seeking the Lord in and above all earthly concerns.

Our contemporary cultural context may urge us not to make moral judgments and to respect the freedom and autonomy of those whose values are different from our own. For example, our society may encourage us to accept the sin of abortion as "the right to choose." In many convincing ways, we may be pressured by society to accept injustice and quiet our consciences about the immoral practices of governments who tolerate the enslavement, maiming, or killing of their minorities, or corporations that make huge profits from unjust labor practices. But the Church teaches that we have a serious responsibility to love our neighbor **(1789)**, and at the same time, an equally serious responsibility to make moral judgments that will work for the common good **(1880)**.

A well-formed Christian moral conscience will recognize as immoral the actions of those who lie, steal, or are violent with others, those who do not discipline their sexual drives, those who deliberately abuse alcohol or drugs, those who direct corporations or governments that engage in unjust practices against individuals or societies, those who act with callous disregard for the physical environment, etc. Note that it is always an attitude, word, or action that is condemned: not the sinner, but the sin itself. The wise adage says, "We should hate the sin but love the sinner."

Sharing Our Faith

- When have I best formed my conscience based on gospel values?
- When has a conflict arisen between my moral convictions and the action of a family member, a friend, or a co-worker? How did I reconcile being loving and caring while addressing the issue?
- Have I ever experienced a time when the demands of civil authorities conflicted with my own conscience? How did I resolve the issue?

Living the Good News

Determine a specific action (individual or group) that flows from your sharing. This should be your primary consideration.

When choosing an individual action, determine what you will do and share it with the group. When choosing a group action, determine who will take responsibility for different aspects of the action.

The following are secondary suggestions:

- Reflect upon one aspect of your life, for example, marriage, family, work, school, leisure, corporate, political, etc. in which you could better live according to a well-formed conscience. Make a decision to change your response to that situation.
- Speak out on behalf of hunger. Contact your local food bank or one of the following:
  Bread for the World
  50 F Street, NW
  Suite 500
  Washington, DC 20001
  Phone   800-82-BREAD or 202-639-9400
  Fax   202-639-9401
  Web site   www.bread.org
  E-mail bread@bread.org
          or
  Catholic Relief Services
  209 West Fayette Street
  Baltimore, MD 21201-3443
  Phone   800-222-0025
              410-625-2220
  Fax   410-685-1635
  Web site   www.catholicrelief.org
  E-mail educationprograms@catholicrelief.org
          or
  Operation Rice Bowl
  200 Noll Place
  Huntington, IN 46750
  Phone   800-222-0025
- Pray for, write, or talk to a person from whom you are estranged.

As my response to the gospel of Jesus, this week I commit to _____

_____ .

Lifting Our Hearts

Pray together

Lord Jesus, through your Church
you teach us that love is our origin,
love is our goal,
and love will be our fulfillment in heaven.
Enlighten our minds and open our hearts
to the many challenges of love in our lives.
Help us to seek you and
find you in one another,
especially in those in need. Amen.

Looking Ahead

- Prepare for your next session by prayerfully reading and studying
  — **Session 4: Virtues**
  — Scripture: Philemon 4-9 ; Ephesians 4:25-32 (Rules for the new life)
  — pages 315-317 on the "Excellence of Virtues," and page 318 on "Loves, Rules, and Grace"" from Chapter 23 "Life in Christ— Part I" of the *United States Catholic Catechism for Adults*

- You may like to consult the relevant paragraphs from the *Catechism of the Catholic Church*:
  — paragraphs 1803-1845 on the virtues

- Remember to use RENEWING FAMILY FAITH (see pages 82-83) and its helpful suggestions on how to extend the fruits of your sharing beyond your group, especially to your families.

Session 4

Virtues

✝✝✝

Suggested environment

Bible, candle, and, if possible, the *Catechism of the Catholic Church*
Begin with a quiet, reflective atmosphere.

Lifting Our Hearts

Song

"Lord, Here I Am," Julienne Johnson and Mark LeVang, *RENEW the Face of the Earth*, Seasons 1 and 2

Pray together

Lord Jesus Christ,
as we seek to live out your will
in our daily lives,
we often become intensely aware
of the wide disparity between what we should be doing
and what we actually find ourselves doing
in our relationships with family members
as well as those with whom we work and play.
By the work of your Holy Spirit,
give us the insight to face the true motives
for our attitudes, words, and actions.
Help us to overcome our selfishness and envy
so that we may be a blessing to others
rather than a stumbling block to their spiritual growth. Amen.

Sharing Our Good News

*Share how you did with your **Living the Good News** from the previous session.*

Exploring the *Catechism*

A virtue is an habitual and firm disposition to do the good. It allows the person not only to perform good acts, but to give the best of himself

[or herself]. **The virtuous person tends toward the good with his [or her] sensory and spiritual powers. The virtuous person pursues the good and chooses it in concrete actions (1803).**

Throughout human history, thinking persons have reflected on the importance of virtues or good habits that make it possible for us to live productive and peaceful lives in society. Christian living involves the development of good habits that direct our attitudes, words, and actions by the power of the Holy Spirit. But good habits do not come easily; they are the result of constant striving and disciplined effort. Bad habits, or vices, need to be overcome as the person seeks to follow more closely the way of the Lord. The more we do good and avoid evil, the more we grow in a joyful outlook and a peaceful heart **(1804).**

There are four moral virtues that play a pivotal role in our lives: prudence, justice, fortitude, and temperance **(1805).** These human virtues become **"purified and elevated"** by God's grace **(1810).** Jesus gives us the help we need to maintain our moral balance in a world that is wounded by sin and selfishness **(1811).**

Prudence guides our consciences to apply moral principles correctly in our daily living **(1806).** Justice disposes our hearts and minds to respect the rights of others and promote harmony and equity in human relationships **(1807).**

Fortitude strengthens us in difficult times and keeps us on the correct path. It helps us to overcome fear and accept the trials and sufferings that come our way **(1808).** Temperance is the mastery we gain over our feelings and appetites, enabling us to maintain a proper balance even in the midst of desires that are inherently insatiable **(1809).**

Christ's gift of salvation offers us the grace necessary to persevere in the pursuit of the virtues. Everyone should always ask for this grace of light and strength, frequent the sacraments, cooperate with the Holy Spirit, and follow his calls to love what is good and shun evil (1811). The human virtues are rooted in the theological virtues, which...are the foundation of Christian moral activity... (1812-1813).

Theological virtues are not acquired or merited by our human efforts but are directly **infused by God into the souls of the faithful to make**

them capable of acting as his children and of meriting eternal life. The theological virtues of faith, hope, and charity change us and make us able to participate in the life of the Holy Trinity **(1813).**

Faith is the theological virtue by which we believe in God and believe all that he has said and revealed to us, and that Holy Church proposes for our belief, because he is truth itself (1814). Hope is the theological virtue by which we desire the kingdom of heaven and eternal life as our happiness, placing our trust in Christ's promises and relying not on our own strength, but on the help of the grace of the Holy Spirit (1817). Charity is the theological virtue by which we love God above all things for his own sake, and our neighbor as ourselves for the love of God (1822).

The virtue of charity animates and inspires all the other virtues in the service of love. Our human ability to believe, to hope, and to love is elevated to a supernatural level by the powerful presence of God's Holy Spirit **(1827, 1830),** giving us abiding gifts and bearing the fruits that will yield fulfillment in eternal glory **(1830, 1832).**

Scripture: Pondering the Word   Ephesians 4:25-32
                                       Philemon 4-9

Sharing Question

- The readings speak of the virtues of truth, integrity, generosity, kindness, sincerity, peace, etc. Who has impressed you with their virtuous life? What virtues are evident in this person?

Exploring the *Catechism* (continued)

God's grace flows from the common action of the three Divine Persons, but we also assign specific tasks to each in order to aid our understanding of the divine action. We say that God the Father created us, Jesus the Son redeemed us, and the Holy Spirit makes us holy. God's presence within us produces certain effects, which we call the theological virtues, namely, faith, hope, and charity. This is how we are enabled to believe in Christ as our Savior, to hope for God's mercy, and to try to serve one another with the love that comes not from our own poor hearts but from the heart of God.

The mystery of the Trinity is at the heart of Christian faith **(234-237).** We express our belief in the Trinity when we make the sign of the cross, when we pray the Apostles' Creed and the Nicene Creed. The doctrine of the Trinity—the three Divine Persons in one God—sheds light on who we are as Christians. The first Letter of John says that God is love (1 John 4:8, 16). Love does not describe a static reality but a dynamic activity. The Divine Persons love one another with an infinite and passionate tenderness (John 3:35, 5:20). The presence of the Holy Spirit dwelling within us places us into the vibrant heart of the loving relationship that exists among the eternal and infinite Persons.

The Holy Spirit enlightens the mind to distinguish altruism from selfishness, good from evil, and manipulation from loving activity. The Spirit sensitizes our feelings about good and evil and strengthens our will to choose good and reject evil. Christ's death on the cross seals the New Covenant, bringing us unconditional forgiveness if we admit our sins and our need for God's forgiveness. Heaven and forgiveness are gifts from God. (grace); they cannot be earned or deserved.

Jesus tells us to love one another in the same way that he has loved us. "No one has greater love than this, to lay down one's life for one's friends" (John 15:13).

Jesus further reminds us: "If you continue in my word, you are truly my disciples; and you will know the truth, and the truth will make you free" (John 8:31-32; see also 17:17, 18:37).

This is how Christ's followers know that morality is all about relationships. As disciples of Jesus, we reverence the truth that comes to us in the Scripture and Sacred Tradition of his Church. We believe we know the truth about moral living, about how we should treat one another in the light of God's revelation.

Sharing Our Faith

- In what ways has the Holy Spirit enlightened my mind and deepened my understanding about good and evil?
- In what area of my life is it most difficult to be totally honest with myself? Why? What can I do about this?
- Reflect on one of the moral virtues and one of the theological virtues. Where do I see each in my life now or in the past? How can I use these to gain strength to tackle difficult moral situations or situations that cause conflict with my conscience?

Living the Good News

Determine a specific action (individual or group) that flows from your sharing. This should be your primary consideration.

When choosing an individual action, determine what you will do and share it with the group. When choosing a group action, determine who will take responsibility for different aspects of the action.

The following are secondary suggestions:

- Read again the section in the *Catechism* that focuses on the virtues (1803-1845). Choose one virtue and ask the Holy Spirit to strengthen this virtue in you. Write steps in your journal or share with a friend how you intend to work to include this virtue in your life more frequently.
- Reflect on the Trinity. Which person of the Trinity do you turn to in times of joy, trouble, confusion, and peace? What draws you to this Person of the Trinity? Journal your feelings or share them with a friend.
- Reflect on the Trinity in relation to the virtues. Draw the image that comes to mind. Consider further expressing that image in a poem, pottery, or photography.

As my response to the gospel of Jesus, this week I commit to _____

_____ .

Lifting Our Hearts

Psalm 3 *(Prayed alternately by two persons or two groups)*

Side 1	O LORD, how many are my foes!
	Many are rising against me;
	many are saying to me,
	"There is no help for you in God."
Side 2	But you, O LORD, are a shield around me,
	my glory, and the one who lifts up my head.
	I cry aloud to the LORD,
	and he answers me from his holy hill.
Side 1	I lie down and sleep;
	I wake again, for the LORD sustains me.
	I am not afraid of ten thousands of people
	who have set themselves against me all around.

| Side 2 | Rise up, O LORD!
    Deliver me, O my God!… |
| Side 1 | Deliverance belongs to the LORD;
    may your blessings be on your people! |

Looking Ahead

- Prepare for your next session by prayerfully reading and studying
  - **Session 5: Sin, Mercy and Moral Solidarity**
  - Scripture: John 4:4-30 (The encounter between Jesus and the Samaritan woman)
  - pages 324-327 on "Consciousness of solidarity and social justice" from Chapter 24 "Life in Christ—Part II: The Principles of the Christian Moral Life" of the *United States Catholic Catechism for Adults*

- You may like to consult the relevant paragraphs from the *Catechism of the Catholic Church*:
  - paragraphs 1846-1876 on "sin"
  - paragraphs 1877-1896 on "the person and society"
  - paragraphs 1897-1927 on "participation in social life"
  - paragraphs 1928-1948 on "social justice"

- Remember to use RENEWING FAMILY FAITH (see pages 82-83) and its helpful suggestions on how to extend the fruits of your sharing beyond your group, especially to your families.

Session 5

Sin, Mercy, and Moral Solidarity

✝✝✝

Suggested environment

Bible, candle, and, if possible, the *Catechism of the Catholic Church*
Begin with a quiet, reflective atmosphere.

Lifting Our Hearts

Song

"Not One Stone," Julienne Johnson, *RENEW the Face of the Earth*,
Seasons 1 and 2

Pray together

> Dear Jesus,
> > Envelop us with your love and mercy.
> > Open us to your Holy Spirit.
> > Heal our hearts wounded by sin.
> > Heal those we have sinned against.
> > Help us to see you in all our sisters and brothers.
> > Teach us to love as you love. Amen.

Sharing Our Good News

*Share how you did with your **Living the Good News** from the previous session.*

Exploring the *Catechism*

Jesus gave us two great commandments: to love God above all else and to love our neighbor as ourselves (Matthew 22:37–40; see Deuteronomy 6:4–5 and Leviticus 19:18). Our understanding of God as a loving community of Persons helps us to recognize that all of us are one human community; as the Church, we are the Body of Christ. Through the Holy Spirit, Jesus shares his own Divine Life with us in grace. Grace enables us to recognize others as sisters and brothers. How, then, could we dare not love one another?

Jesus' love in obedience to his Father's will is our model. His humble obedience stands in stark contrast to the sinful attitudes, words, and actions that seem so often to preoccupy our hearts **(1852-1853)**. The gospel tells of God's mercy given to sinful human beings through Jesus Christ **(1846)**. When we examine our human experience, we recognize our need for God's forgiveness and mercy. The most important prerequisite to our following of Jesus is the fact that we admit our sins and our need of God's forgiveness. The Gospel of Matthew (Matthew 12:31) warns of the sin against the Holy Spirit, which is a belligerent refusal of God's loving mercy **(1864)**.

How do we name sin? Sin is an offense against God, the Ultimate Reality. How do we recognize sin? It is an offense against truth, reason, and right conscience. When we sin, we turn away from God's love for us. Sin is rooted in pride. We make ourselves the norm for right conduct. Sin sets us on a path of alienation from others and from the truth of our own inner being **(1849-1850)**. Sin always expresses the disorder of our nature **(402-409)**.

In addition to original sin, the Church distinguishes other sin as mortal or venial. *Mortal sin* **destroys charity in** [our] **heart**[s]...**by a grave violation of God's law; it turns** [us] **away from God, who is** [our] **ultimate end and** [our] **beatitude, by preferring an inferior good to him (1855)**.

Mortal sin is so serious in its effects **(1861)** that there are three conditions that must be present in order for us to commit such a grievous offense. The matter itself must be a serious violation of God's will for us. We must be fully aware of what we are doing, and we must freely consent to this grave evil **(1857-1860)**.

Venial sin weakens charity (1863). *Venial sin* **allows charity to subsist, even though it offends and wounds it (1855)**. Venial sin does not rupture our connection with God, but it does weaken our relationship with him and others **(1863)**.

Just as virtues are good habits, so vices are evil habits. When personal immorality goes unrestrained, it may give rise to the corruption of human institutions and governments **(1869)**. Sinfulness often begets structures in society that serve violence and injustice.

Scripture: Pondering the Word John 4:4-30

Sharing Question

- Talk about the way Jesus and the Samaritan woman relate to each other. How does this teach me or us to be in right relationship with others?

Exploring the *Catechism* (continued)

Today, in the West, we speak about the intense individualism of society. Individual rights obsess us to the extent that, in some cases, safeguarding these rights defies common sense and militates against the common good. Individual rights are important, but not to the exclusion of what is necessary for the common good.

The **common good is to be understood** as "the sum total of social conditions which allow people, either as groups or as individuals, to reach their fulfillment more fully and more easily" (*Gaudium et spes* 26 § 1; cf. *Gaudium et spes* 74 § 1). **It consists of *three essential elements* (see 1906): First, the common good presupposes *respect for the person*.... Second, the common good requires the *social well-being* and *development* of the group itself.... Finally, the common good requires *peace*, that is, the stability and security of a just order (1907-1909).**

The human person is the bearer of God-given rights that should be supported and protected by society. The principle of solidarity sets limits to the intervention of institutions and government in our lives **(1883-1885)**. Social organizations should conform to the norms of justice and the advancement of the common good **(1888)**. Thus the love of God and of neighbor are ultimately served only by the divine gift of charity that insists on respect for the rights of all members of the human family **(1889-1896)**. In the Scripture we just read, Jesus revealed himself to the Samaritan woman who was not only a woman but also a foreigner. Both women and foreigners were considered to be of "lower status," but Jesus understood that in God's design there is no such thing as "lower status." All are to be respected (see also Galatians 3:28).

Sharing Our Faith

- When, and with whom, have I shared an experience of solidarity?

Exploring the *Catechism* (continued)

Jesus teaches that loving our neighbor is inseparable from loving God.

We are, by nature, social beings, and so need to exchange conversation, goods, and services with one another **(1877-1879)**. We create and sustain community, modeling the loving community of the Trinity. The family and the state are examples of social organization that are necessary to our human development and fulfillment **(1882)**.

It is the role of authority to ensure the common good in society **(1897-1899)**. Since all authority comes ultimately from God, unjust laws are not morally binding **(1903)**. The political community has the obligation to develop, preserve, and protect the common good. We have a moral obligation to become involved in the public life of our community, defending and promoting the rights and dignity of all persons, overcoming sinful inequalities, and enhancing both the socio-economic and the spiritual resources that are essential to our solidarity as human persons **(1905-1948)**.

We are all connected and we are continuing to grow in our understanding of our world as interdependent. Today we speak of the globalization of everything. We recognize that we have one water supply, one air supply. We know if the rain forests are destroyed in South America, the entire world will suffer. **The unity of the human family, embracing people who enjoy equal natural dignity, implies a *universal common good*…[which] is always oriented towards the progress of persons… (1911-1912).**

We all are called to participation in and responsibility for the social order. Participation is achieved by first taking charge of the responsibilities in our own life: family, work, ecology, etc. In addition, it is important to **take an active part in *public life*…. [T]he participation of all in realizing the common good calls for a continually renewed *conversion* of the social partners…. Much care should be taken to promote institutions that improve the conditions of human life (1915-1916).**

It is imperative that we continually strive to balance the rights of individuals with the common good. Individual rights and the common good need always to be defined in reference to one another **(1905)**.

Sharing Our Faith

- How have I contributed to the common good of society?

Exploring the *Catechism* (continued)

We've often heard people say, "It isn't fair." Most of us have had experiences when we were treated unjustly. The *Catechism* tells us that there are three aspects necessary for social justice: respect for the human person, for equality and differences among people, and for human solidarity **(1943-1948).**

Social justice is about "right relationships." There is probably no moral concept as key in the Old Testament as that of justice. We hear over and over about how God is always calling us to be in right relationship with him, with others, and with the world. And we see Jesus always calling others to be in right relationships.

Social justice can be achieved only when we recognize the inherent rights of every person and we realize those rights flow from their dignity as persons or children of God **(1929-1931).** As followers of Jesus, we must give special attention to the dignity of those who are disadvantaged or different from ourselves **(1932-1933).**

The **differences** in people **belong to God's plan.** St. Catherine of Siena (*Dialogues* I, 7) writes that God said to her: "I distribute the virtues quite diversely; I do not give all of them to each person, but some to one, some to others…. And so I have given many gifts and graces, both spiritual and temporal, with such diversity that I have not given everything to one single person, so that you may be constrained to practice charity towards one another…. I have willed that one should need another and that all should be my ministers in distributing the graces and gifts they have received from me" **(1937).**

We know that **[t]here exist also *sinful inequalities* that affect millions of men and women. These are in open contradiction of the Gospel (1938)** and require us to confront the unjust systems that continually support these inequalities **(1939).** For example, many countries put an embargo on trade with South Africa during the time of apartheid, which helped to dismantle this unjust system.

Finally, true social justice requires solidarity—the ability to exist and work together cooperatively. **Socio-economic problems can be resolved only with the help of all the forms of solidarity: solidarity of the poor** among themselves, between rich and poor, of workers among themselves, between employers and employees in a business, solidarity among nations and peoples. International solidarity is a requirement of the moral order; world peace depends in part upon this (1941).

Sharing Our Faith

- Where have I struggled to live in "right relationship"? What role does my faith play in the struggle?
- How have I experienced solidarity in my workplace? In my neighborhood? In my parish?
- What initial steps can I take to further solidarity in these places?

Living the Good News

Determine a specific action (individual or group) that flows from your sharing. This should be your primary consideration.

When choosing an individual action, determine what you will do and share it with the group. When choosing a group action, determine who will take responsibility for different aspects of the action.

The following are secondary suggestions:

- Choose to participate in public life. For example, if you are not registered to vote, do so. If you are not aware of local political issues, find out about them. Write to your representative or congressperson about an issue of concern for the common good.
- Choose an area in your local community or the world community where there is a greater need for solidarity. As a group, select one Living the Good News action that would provide greater solidarity.
- Read, study, and/or watch the video "Communities of Salt and Light" that provides reflections on the social mission of the parish. Available from the
  United States Conference of Catholic Bishops
  3211 4th Street N.E., Washington, D.C. 20017-1194
  Phone: 800-235-8722
  Web site: www.usccb.org
- Decide as a group how you can be in greater solidarity with persons from another country. Pray for these persons and begin to communicate with them in the spirit of sharing your common concerns.

As my response to the gospel of Jesus, this week I commit to _____

_____ .

Lifting Our Hearts

Share spontaneous prayers together.

To conclude, join hands and pray the Our Father, remembering that our world is called to be a community of people with God as our Father.

Looking Ahead

- Prepare for your next session by prayerfully reading and studying
  — **Session 6: Moral Law, Grace, and the Church**
  — Scripture: Colossians 1:3-10
  — pages 327-331 on "God's law as our guide", "Grace and justification", and "The Church as mother and teacher" from Chapter 24 "Life in Christ—Part II: The Principles of the Christian Moral Life" of the *United States Catholic Catechism for Adults*

- You may like to consult the relevant paragraphs from the *Catechism of the Catholic Church*:
  — paragraphs 1949-1986 on the moral law
  — paragraphs 1987-2029 on grace and justification
  — paragraphs 2030-2051 on the Church, as mother and teacher

- Remember to use RENEWING FAMILY FAITH (see pages 82-83) and its helpful suggestions on how to extend the fruits of your sharing beyond your group, especially to your families.

Session 6

Moral Law, Grace, and the Church

✝✝✝

Suggested environment

Bible, candle, and, if possible, the *Catechism of the Catholic Church*
Begin with a quiet, reflective atmosphere.

Lifting Our Hearts

Song

"Renew My Life," Rick Riso, *RENEW the Face of the Earth*, Seasons 1 and 2

Invite one person to pray Psalm 119:33-40 aloud.

Pray together

Lord Jesus Christ,
you promised to be among us
whenever we gather in your name.
We come together now
and ask you to stay with us always.
We are grateful for the gift of your Holy Spirit
dwelling within us.
Fill us with faith in you,
pour hope into our hearts
and help us to love you.
As we are caught up into the dynamism of your divine life,
grant us a share in the energy and peace
of your eternal plan. Amen.

Sharing Our Good News

*Share how you did with your **Living the Good News** from the previous session.*

Exploring the *Catechism*

The moral law is the work of God. It teaches us rules for living that will
lead us to the enjoyment of God's promises **(1950)**. Jesus tells us that he is

the way and the truth and the life (John 14:6). If we follow Jesus' way, we will live moral lives.

In his encyclical, *Veritatis Splendor*, John Paul II reminds us that God created us with a natural desire for goodness. This set of positive inclinations of **natural law is written and engraved in the soul of each and every** [person] **(1954).** St. Thomas Aquinas speaks of natural law being imprinted in our hearts. **"The natural law is nothing other than the light of understanding placed in us by God; through it we know what we must do and what we must avoid. God has given this light or law at the creation"** (St. Thomas Aquinas, *Dec. praec.* I) **(1955).**

Natural law is the foundation for our rights and responsibilities as free persons. As a result, a basic agreement about ethical principles, such as respect for each other's lives, property, and reputation, arises *naturally* whenever people experience themselves as rational human beings. These basic moral values are often articulated by various religious traditions and are commonly accepted by the entire human family. They are essential to our living together in society. The Bible itself mentions this reality as the work of God (Romans 1:20; 2:14) **(1954).**

The natural law provides the solid and unchanging foundation on which we build the structure of moral and ethical rules that make possible our life in community. It is the basis for our civil laws and is articulated by the Old and New Testaments in the divine law given to us by God **(1950-1960).**

The Old Law is the first stage of revealed Law. Its moral prescriptions are summed up in the Ten Commandments (1962). The law of the Old Testament is a preparation for the gospel, the New Law, which comes to us through faith in Jesus Christ.

The New Law or the Law of the Gospel is the perfection here on earth of the divine law, natural and revealed. It is the work of Christ and is expressed particularly in the Sermon on the Mount (1965). [T]he New Law also includes *the evangelical counsels* of poverty, chastity and obedience, which show very clearly the connection between God's law and God's grace **(1973-1986).** It is a law of love, of freedom, and of grace **(1972).**

Scripture: Pondering the Word   Colossians 1:3-10

Sharing Question

- Paul says that the message of truth has taken root in your life. When have I been stretched in a moral way? How do I see this in light of "natural law"? Was I conscious of God's presence in this action?

Exploring the *Catechism* (continued)

Often, we sing the hymn, "Amazing Grace," without understanding the depths of its meaning. From a Catholic perspective, grace touches upon the totality of our life in the world. Grace enables us to experience God's favor and forgiveness, God's power and presence in our lives and in our world. Grace is warmly personal: we have not been saved or set free, we have not been found or enabled to see, by anything other than God. The "amazing" reality is the fact that, by God's overflowing generosity and goodness, we have been given a share in the divine nature, in the very being of God (2 Peter 1:4).

Grace is the free and undeserved favor of God. It is the word we use to describe the sanctifying gift that prepares for the presence of God's Spirit within us, given at our Baptism. Our Baptism incorporates us into the intimacy of the Holy Trinity and enables us to call God our Father. Grace, therefore, is the dynamic foundation of the Christian moral life, helping us to overcome focusing solely on our own perceived needs and desires. By the action of grace, our minds and hearts are sensitized to involve us in the process of conversion, overcoming our resistance to change by shifting our perspective to one of growth in the Spirit.

Grace enables us to leave behind our prejudices and selfishness. Grace gives us the strength to "die to ourselves" or "lay down our lives" in making the difficult choices that will have positive effects on others and on the society. All Christians have a responsibility to spread the good news of God's grace abiding within them. By word and example, we invite others to learn and to share in the marvelous gifts of God's unconditional love for us. We are reminded: **It is in Christ, Redeemer and Savior, that the divine image, disfigured in [us] by the first sin, has been restored to its original beauty and ennobled by the grace of God (1701).** Grace is supernatural, surpassing our human powers of intellect and will, a gift in the most sublime sense of the word **(1996-1999)**. Grace describes the relationship between God and us in which God's love for us draws us into new life, to a life of charity and justice.

Traditionally, the Church has distinguished two main kinds of grace: actual grace and sanctifying grace. Actual graces refer to those moments when God intervenes in our lives to initiate or develop our growth in living a life of holiness, for example, when we feel a prompting within us to perform a charitable act, make a visit to the Blessed Sacrament, or bring a hot meal to a shut-in. God's grace prepares our hearts to receive him. We may freely accept this amazing gift because God will not manipulate or coerce us.

By the habitual gift of sanctifying grace, God enables us in our attitudes, words, and actions, to live out his love in our daily lives. God is present within us and directs our love in reconciling and fruitful ways. Thus, a parent, despite a difficult day at work, comes home each evening and lovingly prepares a meal for the family. Although the effects of grace offer us a guarantee of God's loving presence, we rely on our faith rather than on our feelings **(2000-2005)**.

IF OUR HEARTS DO NOT CONDEMN US WE HAVE BOLDNESS BEFORE GOD
1 John 3.21

Who better serves as our example than Mary? She trusted God even in the face of fear and uncertainty (see Luke 1:26-38). God hears our prayers and often may give us graces and blessings in response to our prayerful requests, but it is the loving goodness of Jesus that is the source of all our merits before God **(2006-2011)**.

The grace of the Holy Spirit confers upon us the righteousness of God. Uniting us by faith and Baptism to the Passion and Resurrection of Christ, the Spirit makes us sharers in his life (2017). The first work of the Holy Spirit is evident in our conversion from sin and our turning toward God. The sacrifice of Christ on the cross has won us justification and established the cooperation between God's grace and human freedom. The Spirit of Christ makes us holy and prepares us for the eternal life that is promised to Christ's faithful followers **(1994-1995)**.

Sharing Our Faith

- What is so amazing about the grace of God in my life?

Exploring the *Catechism* (continued)

All are called to holiness. Spiritual progress brings us into an increasingly intimate union with Jesus. It is often by the way of suffering and self-denial that God's grace works to convert our hearts and call us closer to him. As sinners, we hope for God's mercy, and as those who try every day to listen to God's voice and accomplish his will, we are enabled to hope for the endless joy of heaven **(2018-2029)**.

It is consoling to learn that the Church safeguards **the fundamental rights of the human person** [and] **the salvation of souls (2032).**

When Paul wrote to Timothy, he reminded him and his community how "to behave in the household of God, which is the Church of the living God, the pillar and bulwark of the truth" (1 Timothy 3:15). We hear and must listen to the voice of the Lord in the catechesis, preaching, and moral teaching of the Church, most especially when the Church speaks with infallible authority. Jesus' contemporaries marveled that he spoke with authority and Christ speaks today through his Church in the same way. **The authority of Christ is ensured by the charism of *infallibility* (2035).**

As we tune our ear to hear Christ speak to us in the teaching of the Church, our love deepens for her. She speaks to us with the affection of a mother and disposes us to a life of prayer and good works that will serve God and our neighbor.

The moral life is a spiritual worship. Christian activity finds its nourishment in the liturgy and the celebration of the sacraments (2047). By our commitment to living holy lives, we draw others to believe in Christ and to love as we are loved **(2030-2051).**

Sharing Our Faith

- In what ways does the Holy Spirit enlighten my mind and deepen my understanding about good and evil? What gift of the Holy Spirit helps me in this understanding? Is there a specific good I believe God is inviting me to do or a specific evil God is inviting me to avoid?

Living the Good News

Determine a specific action (individual or group) that flows from your sharing. This should be your primary consideration.

When choosing an individual action, determine what you will do and share it with the group. When choosing a group action, determine who will take responsibility for different aspects of the action.

The following are secondary suggestions:

- Ask God for insight into attitudes you may have that block the action of grace in your life.
- Spend five or ten minutes reviewing your day in the light of God's grace.
- Read and reflect on John Paul II's encyclical, *Veritatis Splendor* (available in bookstores or online: www.usccb.org). Journal the significant ideas for you. Share them with another person.
- If you are not continuing with Session 7 of *Why Catholic?* until later, you may want to use *PRAYERTIME: Faith-Sharing Reflections on the Sunday Gospels,* Cycle A, B, or C and other resources for small groups. (For information, call 908-769-5400; to order, 888-433-3221, www.renewintl.org.)

As my response to the gospel of Jesus, this week I commit to _____

_____ .

Lifting Our Hearts

Take a moment to silently name an area of your life in which you need inspiration and encouragement and grace.

Let us pray silently that the Spirit of God will inspire and encourage us to know and to accomplish the work of the Lord Jesus in our daily lives through grace.

A Psalm of Longing *(Prayed alternately by two persons or two groups)*

Side 1   My Spirit hungers for your love,
                     O Divine Lover of hearts,
                     I long for your presence
                     and the joy of your peace.

Side 2   Teach us what it means to love, O God.
                     Show us all that love includes,
                     Love of self, love of others, love of all the earth,
                     Love of all that you yourself love.

Side 1   Teach us that all of your creation is sacred,
                     And that all of it is loved by you.
                     Remind us often that to love another
                     Is just another way of loving you.

Side 2   Bless all those we love, O God,
                     And help us to love all those you love—
                     The poor, the homeless, those out of work,

	Those different from ourselves.
Side 1	Awaken us to the present moment
	To see the suffering around us.
	If we love you, we shall reach out to those in pain
	As we feel your touch upon our hearts.
Side 2	Move us to action on their behalf
	Let our love extend in kindness.
	Love those we love, dear God,
	And help us to love those you love.
All	Love all those we love, dear God, and help us to love all those you love. Amen.

Looking Ahead

- Prepare for your next session by prayerfully reading and studying
  — **Session 7: Love of God**
  — Scripture: Matthew 19:16-21 (The encounter between Jesus and the rich young man)
  — the summary of doctrinal statements presented by the *United States Catholic Catechism for Adults*:
  for the first commandment, pages 347-8; for the second commandment, page 358; and for the third commandment, pages 369-70

- You may like to consult the relevant chapters from the *United States Catholic Catechism for Adults*
  — Chapter 25 "The First Commandment: Believe in the True God";
  — Chapter 26 "The Second Commandment: Reverence God's Name";
  — Chapter 27 "The Third Commandment; Love the Lord's Day"

- You may also like to consult the relevant paragraphs from the Catechism of the Catholic Church:
  — paragraphs 2052-2082 on the Ten Commandments
  — paragraphs 2083-2141 on the first commandment
  — paragraphs 2142-2167 on the second commandment
  — paragraphs 2168-2195 on the third commandment

- Remember to use RENEWING FAMILY FAITH (see pages 82-83) and its helpful suggestions on how to extend the fruits of your sharing beyond your group, especially to your families.

Session 7

Love of God

†·†·†

Suggested environment

Bible, candle, and, if possible, the *Catechism of the Catholic Church*
Begin with a quiet, reflective atmosphere.

Lifting Our Hearts

Song

"Your Faithful Love," Rick Riso, *RENEW the Face of the Earth,*
Seasons 1 and 2

Invite three participants to read each of the three verses.

Leader	It is difficult today, God, to be faithful to your commands. Implant deep within us a desire to follow your way of love and truth.
All	Lord Jesus, set us ablaze with faith. Anchor us in fidelity to your commandments.
Reader	O God, our Father, you are the center of our lives. Give us the grace always to place you first in our lives. Help us to put our trust in you, and be authentic followers of your Word.
All	Lord Jesus, set us ablaze with faith. Anchor us in fidelity to your commandments.
Reader	O God, our Creator, your name is holy. May our lips and our lives proclaim the sacredness of your presence. Let us reverence you in all creation. Forgive us for the times we take your name in vain or slander another.
All	Lord Jesus, set us ablaze with faith. Anchor us in fidelity to your commandments.
Reader	O God, our Companion, you are the Lord of the Sabbath.

Help us to keep Sunday holy,
participating fully in the celebration of Sunday Eucharist,
and giving witness to our communion in faith.

All   Come Holy Spirit, enter into our gathering space.
Fill us with renewed faith and a fiery zeal
to live committed and heroic lives.
May our hearts burn with love for you, your law,
for life, for justice, and for peace. Amen.

Sharing Our Good News

*Share how you did with your **Living the Good News** from the previous session.*

Exploring the *Catechism*

The first three Commandments of the Decalogue—The Ten Commandments

The first commandment: I am the LORD your God: you shall not have strange gods before me.

The second commandment: You shall not take the name of the LORD your God in vain.

The third commandment: Remember to keep holy the LORD's Day.

The Ten Commandments find their full meaning within the New Covenant. The first three commandments deal with the love of God and our response to that love.

In Jesus' reply to the rich young man, in the following gospel story, he acknowledges the importance of the Ten Commandments, but then goes a step further and unfolds the demands of the Commandments. The Commandments cannot be separated from the evangelical counsels of poverty, chastity, and obedience to which all Christians are called **(2053-2054).**

We know from the promise of Jesus that it is only through the power of the Holy Spirit that we can live out these challenges given to the rich young man. What God commands is made possible by God's grace **(2082).**

Reflect again on the story of the rich young man.

Scripture: Pondering the Word   Matthew 19:16-21

Sharing Question

- How has the grace of God enabled me to live out one of the commandments?

Exploring the *Catechism* (continued)

**"The first commandment embraces faith, hope, and charity..."
(2086). [It] requires us to nourish and protect our faith with prudence and
vigilance, and to reject everything that is opposed to it (2088).**

We cannot accept the teachings of Jesus and the moral teachings of our
Church without the gift of faith. Without faith, life doesn't make sense.

Faith is a grace. "While we acknowl-
edge that the grace of God is mysteri-
ously present in all lives, people all too
often resent this grace. They refuse
change and repentance" (USCCB, *Go
and Make Disciples*, p. 4).

Because we live in a secular age,
developing faith from the perspective of
personal conviction is more imperative
than ever. Today people no longer
"inherit" their faith as they did in the
past. Previously, those who were born
into Catholic families, into Catholic
neighborhoods, or belonged to certain
ethnic groups automatically inherited
the faith. This is not necessarily true
today. How many of us have friends
and family members who were born
into the Catholic faith, but no longer practice it? John Paul II has repeated-
ly called for a new evangelization. The U.S. Bishops in their document *Go
and Make Disciples* pray that "our Catholic people will be set ablaze with a
desire to live their faith fully and share it freely with others" (p. 22).

One of the primary ways to be set ablaze with our faith is through
prayer. **The acts of faith, hope, and charity enjoined by the first commandment are accomplished in prayer. Lifting up the mind toward God
is an expression of our adoration of God: prayer of praise and thanksgiv-
ing, intercession and petition.... "[We] ought always to pray and not lose
heart" (Luke 18:1) (2098).**

Sharing Our Faith

- How easily do I accept the gift of faith? What are the things in my
  life that I place before God?

Exploring the *Catechism* (continued)

The second commandment teaches us to respect God's name **(2142)**. Respect for the name of God is an expression not only of respect for God, but for all sacred reality **(2144)**. We are called not only to respect God's name, but to respect one another's names as well. **God calls each one by name. Everyone's name is sacred. The name is the icon of the person (2158).**

Sharing Our Faith

- How is God's name taken in vain in our world today?

Exploring the *Catechism* (continued)

The third commandment requires that we keep sacred "the Sabbath" **(2168)**. One of the concrete ways that we as Catholics keep the Sabbath sacred is by gathering as parish communities for the Eucharist. In fact, the eucharistic celebration of Christ's Resurrection on the Lord's Day is at the heart of the Church's life. Attendance at Mass on Sundays **observes the moral commandment inscribed by nature in the human heart to render to God an outward, visible, public, and regular worship... (2176).** Participation in the communal celebration of the Sunday Eucharist is a means for all of us to give witness to our communion in faith, hope, and charity and to be in communion with our Triune God, the Father, Son, and the Holy Spirit **(2182)**.

Our presence at Mass not only gives glory to God, but also strengthens the faith of our sisters and brothers. Imagine going to church and finding only a few scattered worshipers there on a Sunday morning. When we are part of a large and enthusiastic congregation, the witness of faith we give to one another enhances our growth in all the Christian virtues.

The third commandment also requires that we look at how we spend our time. Does our life have a good rhythm of work and rest? Do we seriously consider that Sunday is a time for rest? Do we make it "the Lord's Day"? If we cannot rest on Sunday because of a work schedule, do we rest on another day of the week? **The institution of the Lord's Day helps everyone enjoy adequate rest and leisure to cultivate their familial, cultural, social, and religious lives (2184).**

The first three of the Ten Commandments focus on faith, God's love for us, and our response to that love. Nothing can be more important in our lives than God. How do we call God by name?

How do we call one another by name? These are challenging questions for us. We need balance—the balance between work and leisure, the balance between independence and dependence, etc. However, the question is even more basic than that. It is a question of how to remain whole in the midst of the distractions of life, how to stay centered no matter what forces pull us away from our spiritual center, how to put God before all else; in a phrase, how to "let go and let God."

LOVE GOD
WITH ALL
YOUR HEART.
MARK 12.30

Sharing Our Faith

• How do I celebrate the Lord's Day?
• What will I do in the next few weeks to have greater balance in my work and rest, in my "doing" and "being"?

Living the Good News

Determine a specific action (individual or group) that flows from your sharing. This should be your primary consideration.

When choosing an individual action, determine what you will do and share it with the group. When choosing a group action, determine who will take responsibility for different aspects of the action.

The following are secondary suggestions:

• Pray for an increase in faith for yourself and one other person.
• If you have the habit of using God's name in a derogatory or frivolous manner, ask someone to help you become aware and change that habit.
• Think through how you spend Sundays. Set aside some time for prayer, Sunday liturgy, rest, and reaching out to someone in need.

As my response to the gospel of Jesus, this week I commit to _____

_____ .

Lifting Our Hearts

Pray together in faith the prayer of the U.S. bishops, which concludes their document, Go and Make Disciples.

> We pray that our Catholic people will be set ablaze with a desire to live their faith fully and share it freely with others. May their eagerness to share the faith bring a transformation to our nation and, with missionary dedication, even to the whole world. We ask

God to open the heart of every Catholic, to see the need for the Gospel in each life, in our nation and on our planet.

We ask Mary, the one through whom Jesus entered our world, to guide us in presenting Jesus to those who live in our land. May her prayers help us to share in her courage and faithfulness. May they lead us to imitate her discipleship, her turning to Jesus, her love for God and for all. May the compassion that Mary has always reflected be present in our hearts.

We also pray that, like the disciples walking that Easter morning to Emmaus, all Catholics may feel their hearts burning through the presence of Jesus. As those two disciples felt the presence of Jesus in their journey, we ask that the ministry of evangelizing help believers feel anew the presence of Jesus and help others discover his gracious presence.

We pray that the fire of Jesus enkindled in us by God's Spirit may lead more and more people in our land to become disciples, formed in the image of Christ our Savior.

Looking Ahead

- Prepare for your next session by prayerfully reading and studying
  - **Session 8: Family**
  - Scripture: Luke 2:41-52 (the boy Jesus in the Temple)
  - the summary of doctrinal statements presented by the *United States Catholic Catechism for Adults* for the fourth commandment, pages 382-3

- You may like to consult the relevant chapters from the *United States Catholic Catechism for Adults*
  - Chapter 28 "The Fourth Commandment: Strengthen Your Family" from the *United States Catholic Catechism for Adults*

- You may also like to consult the relevant paragraphs from the *Catechism of the Catholic Church*:
  - paragraphs 2196-2257 on the fourth commandment

- Remember to use RENEWING FAMILY FAITH (see pages 82-83) and its helpful suggestions on how to extend the fruits of your sharing beyond your group, especially to your families.

Session 8

Family

†††

Suggested environment

Bible, candle, and, if possible, the *Catechism of the Catholic Church*
Begin with a quiet, reflective atmosphere.

Lifting Our Hearts

Song

"Make Us A Family," Cathy Riso and Mark LeVang, *RENEW the Face of the Earth*, Seasons 1 and 2

Take turns praying each section.

1.   Come, let us draw near to God who formed us,
           Let us love the God who nurtures us.
       Give us compassionate hearts, O God, to share your care,
           and listening hearts to hear of your love.

2.   That we may grow in trusting you,
           and in trusting one another, reveal ourselves.
       For your Good News nourishes us abundantly,
           and in sharing, your nourishment abounds.

3.   For we have heard your voice in thousands of different ways,
           and felt your love from those loving us.
       Give us the courage to love with the love you have given us,
           and bring your peace to those who crave it.

4.   There are those, dear God, who are totally unaware of your love.
           There are those for whom no one shows enough love
               to fill their void.
       Are there empty places in me? Do I have some love
               to share?

(Pause for a moment of reflection.)

5.   There are those whose hunger is as basic as food, or a place
        to lay their heads.
        Sometimes they seem cut off from the rest of us,
        With whom can I share, my God? *(Pause)*

6.   For those who hunger for a listening ear,
            or to feel the love of one's family,
        Is it possible for me to help fill their emptiness? *(Pause)*

7.   For parents anxious, upset about their children,
            for their well-being, for their health, for their future,
            for their life with you, O God.
        Is it possible for me to bring them some rest? *(Pause)*

8.   For all the suffering in our world, because of someone else's neglect,
        Is it possible for me to bear their pain? *(Pause)*

All   In you, O God, all this is possible.

Sharing Our Good News

*Share how you did with your **Living the Good News** from the previous session.*

Exploring the *Catechism*

The fourth commandment: Honor your father and your mother.

The first three commandments, as we have seen, deal with the love of God. The other seven are about love of neighbor. The moral requirements of our human nature are made clearer by their revelation as God's law in the commandments **(2070)**. They state the objective ways we can express our respect for the life and reputation of other human beings, as well as for spouse, and property. The fourth commandment teaches us about how we are to relate with family. It is addressed to children and adults alike: "Honor your father and your mother" (Exodus 20:12; Deuteronomy 5:16), but it likewise expresses the kind of relationships all family members are to have with one another **(2197-2198)**.

Jesus spent his first thirty years in a family environment and during that time learned about love, commitment, and respect. Mary and Joseph loved him and taught him; Jesus in turn loved and respected them and grew in "wisdom and grace."

In some ways, the following gospel story reminds us of misunderstandings and miscommunications in families. Jesus was doing what he knew to be right and yet Mary and Joseph were rightly concerned about his safety.

Scripture: Pondering the Word   Luke 2:41-52

Sharing Question

- When have I experienced a misunderstanding with someone in my family or my community, and how did I resolve it? Did this passage or any other gospel passage inspire me to resolve it amicably?

Exploring the *Catechism* (continued)

The Christian family has been often referred to as **a *domestic church*.** This simply means that as family we are a communion of two or more persons, **a *privileged community*** of faith, hope, and charity **(2204-2206).** The family is the basic unit of society and fulfills its mission to be a domestic church through committed love and prayer. As family, we are called to love one another unselfishly, with affection and understanding, to forgive wrongs, and to live and work together in harmony.

Sometimes as family, we are husband, wife, and children, sometimes a single parent and children, sometimes a single person with an extended family. Sometimes as family we are "fractured." Perhaps the greatest love is experienced in family, but also the greatest pain when vows are broken and love disintegrates. Whatever our circumstances, we are called to live in harmony and love.

Parents have the duty to love and respect **their children as *children of God* and...*human persons* (2222)** and to provide *for their physical and spiritual needs* as well as for their education **(2228).** Over the past years, we have seen a significant increase in child abuse and neglect, even child abandonment. There is such a great need to respect and care for children and to advocate for children's rights.

The family is not an isolated unit, but a part of society and thus is responsible for the transformation of the world. A **home is the natural environment for** helping people learn **solidarity and communal responsibilities (2224).**

The transformation of the world...comes about in the quiet home of all life, the family. It comes whenever people understand that the true meaning of love is not the will to dominate, to exploit and to possess; but that it lies in service, generosity, sacrifice, willingness to change and a desire that others be blessed and brought closer to God. When [people] can emerge from the quiet and solitude of their homes touched and renewed by true love, a love that sanctifies us and helps us find the way to heaven, then our land and our people will be blessed, and we will have the strength to face whatever lies ahead.

Alfred Delp, S.J., *On Elizabeth of Hungary*,
source unknown

Sharing Our Faith

- What are some of the relationship struggles I have with young children and teenagers? What aspect of my faith helps me through these situations?

Exploring the *Catechism* (continued)

The fourth commandment reminds grown children of their *responsibilities toward their parents*...**they must give them material and moral support in old age and in times of illness, loneliness, or distress (2218).** We have entered a new time in history in which people are living longer and require care from their grown children. We have a "double standard" for elderly people. On one hand, our culture disregards those who are no longer "productive." With the busy lives we lead, caring for parents can even feel like a burden. On the other hand, many of our resources are used for those who are aging and all of us long to see the elderly cared for well in their old age.

The fourth commandment is clear. We are to honor and care for our parents. Ideally, the family is where all its **members learn to care and take responsibility for the young, the old, the sick, the handicapped, and the poor (2208).**

It is not always possible for an individual family to provide all the help it needs. Thus it is important for society to help care for the needs of everyone **(2208).** When the fourth commandment says, "Honor your mother and father," it extends to the relationship of pupils to their teachers, employees to their employers, citizens to their countries as well as to those who hold positions of authority **(2199).** We are to honor and respect one another.

Those who exercise civil authority are called to do so as a service and not to "lord it over others" (see Matthew 20:25). **No one can command or** establish what is contrary to the dignity of persons and the natural law **(2235)**. In turn, [i]t is the *duty of citizens* to contribute along with the civil authorities to the good of society in a spirit of truth, justice, solidarity, and freedom **(2239)**. Political rights are to be granted to each person according to the requirements of the common good and are to be exercised for the human community **(2237)**.

We are called to be family in society as well as with our biological or adoptive families. We are called to love one another unconditionally in the ways that God loves each of us. We are called to participate in our country and our world as citizens of the same family. Yet the *Catechism* cautions us: **The citizen is obliged in conscience not to follow the directives of civil authorities when they are contrary to the demands of the moral order, to the fundamental rights of persons or the teachings of the Gospel (2242).**

Sharing Our Faith

- What lesson can we learn from Mary and Joseph's parenting style?
- When have I followed my conscience and spoken for or against a civic issue?
- How do I act as servant in my relationships with my family? With those at work? With my friends? If I have sick, elderly, or dependent parents or other family members, what are some of my struggles? What can I do to ease their struggles?

Living the Good News

Determine a specific action (individual or group) that flows from your sharing. This should be your primary consideration.

When choosing an individual action, determine what you will do and share it with the group. When choosing a group action, determine who will take responsibility for different aspects of the action.

The following are secondary suggestions:

- Contact a family member with whom you have lost contact.
- Spend a quiet evening with your family, sharing what it means to be

family to one another; if you are not with your family, choose to spend a quiet evening with a close friend.

- Select one action you could do to help support a family in one of their struggles. For example, offer to take a young child for a day from a parent who is under stress, or visit a nursing home and make a lonely, elderly person a part of your family.
- Teach a child to be involved in a social justice issue.
- Determine how you can be an advocate for children's rights and act on your decision.

As my response to the gospel of Jesus, this week I commit to _____

_____ .

Lifting Our Hearts

Share spontaneous petitions for your family and for society.

Pray together

God, our Father, you watch over us tenderly.
Teach us what it means to have a compassionate heart.
The most expressed virtues of Jesus, your Son,
who came to teach us about you,
were compassion and forgiveness.
How often we forget these virtues
in dealing with those we love the most!
Help us to be compassionate and forgiving
with the members of our own family. Grant us the grace
to be patient with the elderly,
loving toward the little ones,
and understanding with teenagers.
Help us to see the virtue
of being gentle with ourselves,
so we can be gentle with others.
We ask this through Jesus Christ our Lord. Amen.

To conclude, offer each other a sign of God's peace.

Looking Ahead

- Prepare for your next session by prayerfully reading and studying
  — **Session 9: Safeguarding Life and Truth**

- Scripture: Matthew 5:21-24, 38-42, and 43-48 (Jesus' teaching about anger, retaliation, and love of enemies)
- the summary of doctrinal statements presented by the *United States Catholic Catechism for Adults*: for the fifth commandment, pages 400-401; for the eighth commandment, pages 436-437

- You may like to consult the relevant chapters from the *United States Catholic Catechism for Adults*
  - Chapter 29 "The Fifth Commandment: Promote the Culture of Life"
  - Chapter 32 "The Eighth Commandment: Tell the Truth"

- You may also like to consult the relevant paragraphs from the *Catechism of the Catholic Church*:
  - paragraphs 2258-2330 on the fifth commandment
  - paragraphs 2464-2513 on the eighth commandment

- Remember to use RENEWING FAMILY FAITH (see pages 82-83) and its helpful suggestions on how to extend the fruits of your sharing beyond your group, especially to your families.

Session 9
Safeguarding Life and Truth

✝✝✝

Suggested environment

Bible, candle, and, if possible, the *Catechism of the Catholic Church*
Begin with a quiet, reflective atmosphere.

Lifting Our Hearts

Song

"It First Must Begin With Me," Norma Wedewer and Mark LeVang,
RENEW the Face of the Earth, Seasons 1 and 2

(Prayed alternately by two people or two groups)

Side 1	Jesus, teach us what it means to love. You laid down your life for us, but it can be so easy for us to ignore the suffering of others. Much of the world is oppressed and at war for some reason or other, yet we can be so complacent.
Side 2	We need, O God, to realize that we are all our neighbors' keeper, and are responsible for one another. We need to become more conscious of the fact that you regard human life as sacred. We have no right to throw it away for any reason.
Side 1	We need to do more about those who are oppressed and suffering, whether a child, a senior citizen, a teenage mom, someone who is out of a job, someone who is homeless, someone who is hungry. Where do we begin, O God?
Side 2	Peace does begin with me, and so often, I fail to realize it. From this moment forward, dear God, bring to my consciousness your love for life, whenever I am so disturbed as to forget your peace. Help me to be a peacemaker.
All	Put into our hearts some ways of alleviating the evils that destroy peace. Let us bring the blessing of peace to all those with whom we come into contact. Amen.

Sharing Our Good News

*Share how you did with your **Living the Good News** from the previous session.*

Exploring the *Catechism*

The fifth commandment: You shall not kill.

The eighth commandment: You shall not bear false witness against your neighbor.

In his Sermon on the Mount, Jesus recalls the commandment, **"You shall not murder"** (Matthew 5:21), and adds to it a prohibition against **anger, hatred, and vengeance.** He goes even further and **asks his disciples to turn the other cheek,** [and] **to love their enemies (2262).** What a challenging way for us to live! Let's listen to the words of Jesus.

Scripture: Pondering the Word   Matthew 5:21-24, 38-42, and 43-48

Sharing Question

- What is one of my greatest struggles with anger, resentment, hatred or vengeance? How does this passage or any other Scripture passage help me in this struggle?

Exploring the *Catechism* (continued)

Human life is sacred because it is the creation of God. The unborn child, the sick, the elderly, the dying, the condemned criminal all bear the imprint of God's love and likeness. We need to respect the dignity of every life. No one has the right to destroy human life **(2258).** Often the values of society are at odds with the values of the gospel.

We see no greater evidence of this than in the struggle to support the sacredness of life from the moment of conception to the moment of death. Today we are facing serious questions about the sacredness of life and are often confronted with what may seem like "legitimate" reasons for taking a human life. Intentional homicide, abortion, euthanasia, and suicide are directly opposed to the sacredness of life. Legitimate self-defense is morally acceptable, providing the person does not use more violence than necessary **(2263-2267),** while intentional killing is never acceptable **(2268-2269).**

The *Catechism of the Catholic Church* discusses this in the context of the fifth commandment. It exhorts us to avoid anger, hatred, and vengeance. [T]**he traditional teaching of the Church does not exclude recourse to the death penalty, if this is the only possible way of effectively defending human** lives against the unjust aggressor (2267). However, it also cautions that if **non-lethal means are sufficient to defend and protect people's safety from the aggressor, authority will limit itself to such means… (2267).** The *Catechism* says methods of punishment that do not involve the taking of human life are always to be preferred **as these are more in keeping with the concrete conditions of the common good and more in conformity with the dignity of the human person (2267).** In St. Louis, John Paul II illuminated this teaching when he said, "A sign of hope is the increasing recognition that the dignity of human life must never be taken away, even in the case of someone who has done great evil."

We live in a society that also supports the concept that an embryo is not a human life. But our Church teaches that **[h]uman life must be respected and protected absolutely from the moment of conception** since that is the first moment of the person's existence **(2270). Since the first century the Church has affirmed the moral evil of every procured abortion. This teaching has not changed and remains unchangeable. Direct abortion, that is to say, abortion willed either as an end or a means, is gravely contrary to the moral law (2271).**

In light of the same value of the sacredness of life, **direct euthanasia,** which puts **an end to the lives of handicapped, sick, or dying persons,** is not morally acceptable **(2277).** At the same time, discontinuing medical procedures that are **burdensome, dangerous, extraordinary, or… "overzealous"** for persons who are dying may be morally acceptable **(2278).**

As a rule, we should accept medical procedures that offer the possibility of healing. On the other hand, we should reject procedures that serve only to prolong the dying process. Ideally, the decision for extraordinary means of treatment is left up to the individual whose reasonable will must be respected **(2276–2279).** Patients may use a document such as a living will or an advance health directive in order to inform family and physicians about their morally legitimate desire to refuse "extraordinary means" of prolonging life and to help prepare for death.

Suicide is a sad and terrible experience for families and friends of the person. While suicide contradicts the natural inclination toward self-preservation and is in opposition to the legitimate love of self, the Church recognizes grave psychological disturbances that can diminish the responsibility of the one who commits suicide **(2280–2283).**

Another grave issue connected with the sacredness of life is safeguarding peace and avoiding war. **Because of the evils and injustices that accompany all war, the Church insistently urges everyone to prayer and** to action so that the divine Goodness may free us from the ancient bondage of war (2307). While there may be some *legitimate defense by military force,* we must recognize that there is grave danger in modern warfare because it provides the opportunity to those who possess modern scientific weapons to commit serious crimes against innocent people (2307–2317).

In addition, **"[t]he arms race is one of the greatest curses on the human race and the harm it inflicts on the poor is more than can be endured"** (*Gaudium et spes* 81 § 3). **"Blessed are the peacemakers, for they shall be called** [children] **of God"** (Matthew 5:9) **(2329-2330).**

Sharing Our Faith

- What action can I take to support the sacredness of life? What opportunities are presented to me in my daily encounters?
- What have been the effects of modern warfare and the arms race on the poor and the victims of war?

Exploring the *Catechism* (continued)

The eighth commandment calls us to live the truth. Through Jesus, we learn the truth about God and the ways to walk in the reign of God. Jesus tells us, "I am the way, and the truth, and the life" (John 14:6). As disciples of Jesus, we continue in his word so as to know "the truth [that] will make [us] free" (John 8:31-32). As disciples, we learn the unconditional love of the truth **(2464, 2466).**

Lying is the most direct offense against the truth (2483). The true **purpose of speech is to communicate known truth to others (2485).** Too often language is used to obscure the truth. This manipulation leads us to doubt others' words and the integrity of the person. God is best revealed in human relationships that are loving, honest, and just.

In remembrance of Me
SEEK THE TRUTH

By learning to trust others whom we can see, hear, and touch, we may learn to trust God. As we put our faith in the truth that others tell us, we may find it easier to have faith in the truth that God has revealed to us in the Church and in the Scriptures.

The **deliberate intention of leading** someone **into error by saying things contrary to the truth** is **a failure in** both **justice and charity (2485).** We can fail various ways in telling the truth. False witness and perjury are particularly detrimental because they **compromise the exercise of justice (2476).** Giving friends and neighbors due respect for their reputations is also essential. To simply pass on some "gossip" or make negative statements against our neighbors can offend against both charity and justice **(2475-2487).**

Sharing Our Faith

- In what area of my life is it most difficult to be totally honest with myself? Why?

Exploring the *Catechism* (continued)

In addition to challenging us to tell the truth in our individual lives, our *Catechism* reflects on the responsibility of social communications (the media) to also tell the truth. We are at a unique moment in our human history. We have entered an "Age of Communications" in which media play a major role in information, cultural promotion, and formation, and have a major influence on public opinion **(2493).**

The information provided by the media is at the service of the common good (2494). We are living in a graced time in which global communication gives us the opportunity to grow more fully in becoming a world community. It is paradoxical that while communication can be such a wonderful blessing for us as a human community, it can also cause a great deal of distrust and be an instrument of strong negative influences.

Because some of society's media coverage is based on sensationalism and values that are not in tune with the gospel, we need to be vigilant about what we read, listen to, and watch. Most importantly, we need to reflect seriously on what we see and hear and not form our consciences on false or **unwholesome influences (2496).**

> Many research studies have been done to show how the media can influence people. If we are constantly bombarded by values that say "getting ahead" in business at any cost is acceptable, how will we internalize the words of Jesus to "not lord it over one another"? If the media constantly present sexuality as separate from love and commitment, how will we grow to respect the sacredness of our bodies and learn how to love one another? If we see deceit and "getting away with stealing" glamorized, how will

we learn truth and honesty? If we constantly see violence, how will we learn respect for others and the importance of peace?

Sharing Our Faith

- We are called as Christians to witness to the truth of the gospel of Jesus. Through this witness, we transmit our faith in both words and deeds **(2472)**. When have we witnessed to our faith in Jesus in our words or actions?
- What values do the media express? How do these support or oppose the values of Jesus?
- What can I do to challenge the media to greater honesty and integrity?

Living the Good News

Determine a specific action (individual or group) that flows from your sharing. This should be your primary consideration.

When choosing an individual action, determine what you will do and share it with the group. When choosing a group action, determine who will take responsibility for different aspects of the action.

The following are secondary suggestions:

- Consider joining your local Right-to-Life organization.
- Contact the Secretariat for Pro-Life Activities for information on supporting life issues. Decide how you can support life.
  Secretariat for Pro-Life Activities
  United States Conference of Catholic Bishops
  3211 Fourth Street, N.E., Washington, DC 20017-1194
  Phone: 202-541-3070
  Fax: 202-541-3054
  Web site: www.usccb.org/prolife
- Learn about advanced directives for healthcare. Let your doctor and relatives know your wishes.
- Offer assistance to a pregnant woman who is struggling to have her baby or a group home that supports pregnant women.
- Write to television networks and supporting sponsors when you find programs or commercials offensive because of violence, explicit sexuality, pornography, etc.
- Confront and boycott stores that sell pornographic materials.
- Monitor your children's television programs and Internet activities.
- Read, foster, and promote newspapers or magazines that have integrity.

- Contact RENEW International about ordering one or all of the following books: *Embracing Life* by Rev. Michael Mannion, *Make Media Work for You* by June Dwyer Castano, or *Reflections on "Dead Man Walking"* by Sr. Helen Prejean, C.S.J. and Lucille Sarrat. To order: 888-433-3221; Web site: www.renewintl.org.

As my response to the gospel of Jesus, this week I commit to _____

_____ .

Lifting Our Hearts

Take turns praying the following Intercessions for Life. All respond, Lord, hear our prayer.

> For all children who have died from abortion,
> that God might cradle them in his arms
> and grant them eternal peace with him;
> we pray to the Lord...*R.*

> For mothers,
> especially those wracked with fear,
> depression or despair,
> that the new life of their child
> may touch them with the eternal love of God;
> we pray to the Lord...*R.*

> For fathers,
> especially those who are very young,
> that through the intercession of Saint Joseph,
> they might assume the great responsibility
> which God has given to them;
> we pray to the Lord...*R.*

> For the bishops and priests of our Church,
> that by their commitment to the innocent child,
> the Gospel of Life might be preached
> in each of our churches;
> we pray to the Lord...*R.*

> For the justices of our Supreme Court,
> and the legislators of our Congress,
> that the silent voice of the unborn child,
> might move their hearts and minds;
> we pray to the Lord...*R.*

For the children of our country,
especially those who are forgotten or neglected,
that their presence might remind us
of the infinite value of human life;
we pray to the Lord...*R.*

For doctors, nurses and other medical personnel,
especially those tempted by abortion,
that God might change their hearts
and give them the conviction
of the Gospel of Life;
we pray to the Lord...*R.*

Adapted from *Respect Life 2000 Liturgy Guide*
Secretariat for Pro-Life Activities, USCCB, Washington, DC

To conclude, pray the Our Father and offer each other a sign of God's peace.

Looking Ahead

- Prepare for your next session by prayerfully reading and studying
  — **Session 10: Chastity and Love**
  — Scripture: John 15:9-17 ("Love one another as I have loved you")
  — the summary of doctrinal statements presented by the *United States Catholic Catechism for Adults*: for the sixth commandment, pages 426-427; for the ninth commandment, pages 444-445
  - You may like to consult the relevant chapters from the *United States Catholic Catechism for Adults*
  — Chapter 30 "The Sixth Commandment: Marital Fidelity"
  — Chapter 33 "The Ninth Commandment: Practice Purity of Heart"
  - You may also like to consult the relevant paragraphs from the *Catechism of the Catholic Church*:
  — paragraphs 2331-2400 on the sixth commandment
  — paragraphs 2514-2533 on the ninth commandment

- Remember to use RENEWING FAMILY FAITH (see pages 82-83) and its helpful suggestions on how to extend the fruits of your sharing beyond your group, especially to your families.

Session 10
Chastity and Love

†††

Suggested environment

Bible, candle, and, if possible, the *Catechism of the Catholic Church*
Begin with a quiet, reflective atmosphere.

Lifting Our Hearts

Song

"I Commit My Life to You," Mark LeVang and Norma Wedewer, *RENEW the Face of the Earth*, Seasons 3 and 4

Pray together

Loving God,
we ask for your grace and strength
to live lives of chastity and love.
Help us to reverence others and ourselves.
Instill in us a desire
to respond to your grace
and to be selfless and integrated
in our love for others. Amen.

Sharing Our Good News

*Share how you did with your **Living the Good News** from the previous session.*

Exploring the *Catechism*

The sixth commandment: You shall not commit adultery.

The ninth commandment: You shall not covet your neighbor's wife [or husband].

As disciples of Jesus, we believe love is the foundation of all the commandments. When we reflect on the sixth and ninth commandments that speak about human sexuality, the underpinnings, then, are love. God's exuberant love showered great dignity on the human person. God made us good. God made us whole persons and sexuality is a true gift.

All the baptized are called to chastity. Chastity is about reverence. To be chaste is to refrain from illegitimate genital sexual activity, to experience people and all of life in a way that does not violate them or us. To live in a chaste manner means integrating our spiritual and bodily reality. **All...are called to lead a chaste life in keeping with their particular states of life.** Those who are married **are called to live conjugal chastity (2348-2349).**

Maturity is the ability to take personal responsibility for one's attitudes, words, and actions. Sexuality, in its maturity, concerns loving with integrity. It is about giving oneself over to family, friends, community, creativity, work, service to others, delight, joy, God. *Sexuality* **affects all aspects of the human person in the unity of** [one's] **body and soul. It especially concerns affectivity, the capacity to love and to procreate, and in a more general way the aptitude for forming bonds of communion with others (2332).**

God has given us a tremendous sexual energy. This God-given energy is designed for good, healthy, and life-giving relationships. Our sexual energy is not limited to sexual intercourse. We also express it in a broad range of human activity. Meaningful work in the service of others is a healthy way to express the powerful sexual energy God has given us. Building the human family involves the development of personal and committed relationships with the poor and the needy. This is characterized by dedicated service and sacrificial love.

Sexuality is also an important aspect of our relationship with God. The process of accepting our sexuality helps us to be in touch with our true selves, enabling us to be dynamic and honest in our communication with God and in other close relationships. Accepting the fact that we are sexual beings helps us to gain a humble awareness of our own weakness, neediness, and dependence upon the patient mercy of the Lord. Our experience of trying to live a chaste life teaches us to be patient, forgiving, and loving with one another, as God is patient, forgiving, and loving to us.

For married persons, sharing in or abstaining from sexual intercourse for altruistic reasons may be the most profound and meaningful expression of their personal identity, of who they really are. On the other hand, sexual energy directed selfishly obscures life-giving values.

Sexual intercourse motivated solely by selfish desires can lead to immature relationships and poor marital choices, which, in turn, may lead to emptiness, loneliness, and frustration.

Marital commitment involves a man and a woman who are mature enough to make the loving sacrifices that marriage entails. Spouses use their sexual energy to develop a committed, intimate, loving relationship in marriage. The sharing of genital sexuality is the language of committed, abiding, and exclusive love. **Sexuality...becomes personal and truly human when it is integrated into the relationship of one person to another, in the complete and lifelong mutual gift of a man and a woman (2337).**

Sexual fidelity to one's spouse means resisting the sexual allurement of others. Such resistance can only be the result of habits of self-discipline and openness to God's grace.

The model wife or husband manifests the marvelous combination of strength and vulnerability, as well as sensitivity and resolute commitment. The ability to express emotion, and, at the same time, to control its inappropriate expression, is a talent that is learned, often only after countless misjudgments and mistakes. Honest and affectionate communication, understanding, and acceptance are the strong foundation of a healthy marriage.

The Commandments and Church teachings, especially in sexual matters, can seem difficult if taken as sterile prescriptions of what is forbidden. To fully embrace the Commandments and Church teachings, we need to have a strong, loving relationship with our Lord and Savior, who is the way, the truth, and the life (John 14:6). To embrace Jesus is to totally trust the life-giving way he shows us. It is then we discover the reality of grace. Jesus said, "I came that they may have life and have it abundantly" (John 10:10). John's Gospel tells us many ways that Jesus loved. Let's listen to Jesus' description of the ways a disciple is to love.

Scripture: Pondering the Word   John 15:9-17

Sharing Question

- In the Gospel of John, we are challenged to love one another as God loves us. What are some of the things that help us to form healthy relationships with others?

Exploring the *Catechism* (continued)

Through married love, a man and a woman give themselves totally to each other. Married, sexual love is a beautiful gift from God and "concerns the innermost being of the human person..." (*Familiaris consortio* II) **(2361).** Through Matrimony, the wife and husband **are no longer two; from now on they form one flesh. The covenant they freely contracted imposes on**

the spouses the obligation to preserve it as unique and indissoluble (2364). "Therefore what God has joined together, let no one separate" (Mark 10:9).

In married love there are two goals of sexuality—mutual love and procreation. Safeguarding both aspects of sexuality is essential because spouses share in both the love and creative power of God **(2364-2372).** At first glance, the use of artificial contraception would seem to enhance the goal of expressing mutual love by freeing the couple for spontaneous sexual encounters while avoiding the possibility of conceiving a child. But true sexual freedom can be realized only within a context of mutual discipline, loving commitment, and personal responsibility.

When sexual intercourse is free from any of the constraints of personal responsibility and loving commitment, it becomes merely the occasion of personal pleasure achieved with the help of another. When the pursuit of one partner's personal pleasure becomes the primary focus of sexual expression, the entire structure of the marriage is seriously weakened. It becomes no longer the earthly sign of the loving self-sacrifice that images the relationship between Christ and his bride, the Church.

Taking the marriage bond lightly is opposed to Christian values because the marriage covenant between baptized Christians is the sacramental witness of Christ's fidelity to his Church. **Through conjugal chastity,** [the married couple] **bear witness to this mystery before the world (2365).**

Living a sexually moral life is a challenge for everybody, of whatever religion or culture. This means single persons, married persons, celibate persons, young persons, old persons, etc. It is difficult to develop good moral standards concerning sexuality today because sexual mores are frequently debased and the sexual act is so often removed from love.

We have only to read newspapers or watch television or movies to recognize that sex and love have come to be viewed as very separate entities.

Living a life of Christian chastity is a grace-filled response to the call of God. The teaching of the Church as well as the support of family members, good friends, or a small Christian community can be very helpful in this regard. They strengthen us from being unduly influenced by values in our culture opposed to this wonderful gift. In a committed, covenantal relationship, the sexual act is sacramental and brings the married couple to the depths of love and gratitude as well as opens them to be a blessing to each other and to the world. Ideally, it makes them more generous, patient, and loving with each other, with their children, and with others.

Christ's teachings on sexuality are a radical departure from the often-debased sexual practices of the secular world. The Church calls unmarried persons, including homosexual persons, single persons, and vowed religious to abstain from genital activity. The graced effort to live a chaste life, despite enormous difficulties and human weakness, communicates the moral values that Jesus taught. Jesus' teachings provide a great dignity and focus for human sexuality as the foundation for the unconditional love, patient mercy, and abiding faithfulness that are the ideal characteristics both of family life and of God's relationship with his people.

Christian morality is taught and lived within the context of faith, hope, and love. These virtues enable our response to moral teachings. Our *Catechism* instructs us on the importance of living an upright life rather than a double life **(2338).** Sins such as adultery, promiscuity, fornication, prostitution, and rape are obviously opposed to the demands of love **(2353-2356).**

The Church's teachings on issues such as extramarital and premarital sex are particularly at odds with the world's values and often cause tension for those sincerely trying to practice their faith. **Those who are *engaged to marry* are called to live chastity in continence. They should see in this time of testing a discovery of mutual respect, an apprenticeship in fidelity, and the hope of receiving one another from God. They should reserve for marriage the expressions of affection that belong to married love. They will help each other grow in chastity (2350).**

The Church teaches a positive attitude toward the human body, while not losing its awareness of the body's potential for manipulation, sadism, abuse, and control. It is important to get beyond the negative prescriptions and come to a full appreciation of the positive and life-giving aspects of the Church's teaching **(2366-2372).** The positive teachings of the Catholic faith can be both attractive and deeply meaningful.

Sharing Our Faith

- How do the virtues of faith, hope, and love help me to embrace a life of Christian chastity?
- What insights can I offer regarding how Catholic teaching on sexuality calls for a healthy generosity and unselfishness compared to self-centered tendencies in our culture?
- How do I see my sexuality as a gift from God?
- How am I trying to live a chaste life today? What are some of the supports I need to live a chaste life?

Living the Good News

Determine a specific action (individual or group) that flows from your sharing. This should be your primary consideration.

When choosing an individual action, determine what you will do and share it with the group. When choosing a group action, determine who will take responsibility for different aspects of the action.

The following are secondary suggestions:

- If you are married, attend a Marriage Encounter, a retreat, a workshop, or some other gathering to support your spiritual growth as a married couple.
- If you are single, attend a retreat or a gathering with others who are single to support your spiritual journey.
- If you are engaged, attend an Engaged Encounter or a Pre-Cana Conference to prepare for your marriage. Ask your parish priest or a staff person for information.
- Take steps to speak out against pornography or immoral sexuality on television or on the Internet.
- Take time to support a married couple or a single person this week through a phone call, letter, or e-mail.
- In your journaling, pay close attention to the joys and difficulties of your sexuality. Bring these insights to your prayer this week, giving thanks to God for this gift.

As my response to the gospel of Jesus, this week I commit to _____

_____ .

Lifting Our Hearts

Offer spontaneous prayer. Conclude with the Our Father.

End the session by affirming one another. Take time to say one affirming thing about each person in the group. Then give each other a sign of peace.

Looking Ahead

- Prepare for your next session by prayerfully reading and studying
  — **Session 11: On Earthly Goods, Love for the Poor, and Work**
  — Scripture: Luke 19:1-10 (the encounter between Jesus and Zaccheus)
  — the summary of doctrinal statements presented by the *United States Catholic Catechism for Adults* for the seventh commandment, page 426

- You may like to consult the relevant chapters from the *United States Catholic Catechism for Adults*
  — Chapter 31 "The Seventh Commandment: Do Not Steal—Act Justly"

- You may also like to consult the relevant paragraphs from the *Catechism of the Catholic Church*:
  — paragraphs 2401-2463 on the seventh commandment

- Remember to use RENEWING FAMILY FAITH (see pages 82-83) and its helpful suggestions on how to extend the fruits of your sharing beyond your group, especially to your families.

Session 11

On Earthly Goods, Love for the Poor, and Work

✝✝✝

Suggested environment

Bible, candle, and, if possible, the *Catechism of the Catholic Church* *Begin with a quiet, reflective atmosphere.*

Lifting Our Hearts

Song

 "I'll Follow Jesus," Tony Galla, *RENEW the Face of the Earth*, Seasons 3 and 4

Pray together

O Father, Creator of all,
transform us into the image of your Son.
May we put on the mind of Christ.
May our hands be those of Christ.
Dear God, give us the conviction
that the world was created as a gift from you for all.
To live in peace, joy, and harmony
means it is essential that all the goods of the earth be shared.
Help us, O Holy Spirit,
to change our selfish attitudes.
Sometimes we want to blame the victims,
those who are suffering.
Teach us compassion for all hurting people.
Change us into yourself.
Teach us to use the world's goods respectfully.
Help us to share.
We ask this in Jesus' name. Amen.

Sharing Our Good News

*Share how you did with your **Living the Good News** from the previous session.*

Exploring the *Catechism*

The seventh commandment: You shall not steal.

The seventh commandment forbids unjustly taking or keeping the goods of one's neighbor.... It also forbids wronging our neighbor **in any way with respect to his** [or her] **goods. It commands justice and charity in the care of earthly goods and the fruits of** [people's] **labor. For the sake of the common good, it requires respect for the universal destination of goods and respect for the right to private property. Christian life strives to order this world's goods to God and to fraternal charity (2401).**

Creation is an act of all three Persons of the Blessed Trinity. One of the key concepts in the teachings of the Church is that the goods of creation are not given for the few but are destined for everyone and for all of creation. The original gift of the earth to all humanity is the foundation of the right to our private property, but it is essential that the goods of the earth be shared for the common good **(2402-2405).**

In economic matters, respect for human dignity requires the practice of the virtue[s] **of** *temperance...justice...*[and] *solidarity* **(2407).** [A]ny **form of unjustly taking and keeping the property of others is against the seventh commandment:** for example, **deliberate retention of goods lent or of objects lost; business fraud; paying unjust wages; forcing up prices by taking advantage of the ignorance or hardship of another (2409).**

There are different kinds of theft and dishonesty. We are forbidden to take things that are unjustly ours in our personal lives, in our business interactions, in our neighborhoods or in any other aspect of our lives. If we make a promise or a contract, we are bound to keep it. As Christians, we are called to safeguard property rights, pay our debts, and fulfill any obligations freely contracted **(2411).** When we have taken something that is unjustly ours we are called to make *reparation for [the] injustice* **committed** and restore stolen goods to the rightful owner **(2412).**

In the Scriptures, Zacchaeus is a person who came to understand through the power of Jesus that he was to be in "right relationship" with those who were poor and share the earthly goods he had. Jesus blesses Zacchaeus for his pledge: "[I]f I have defrauded anyone of anything, I will pay back four times as much" (Luke 19:8). Those persons who, directly or indirectly have unjustly taken possession of the goods of another, are obliged to make restitution of them **(2412)**.

The seventh commandment also requires respect for all of creation. **Animals, like plants and inanimate beings, are by nature destined for the common good... (2415).** St. Francis of Assisi has always been a saint associated with love for animals and all of the earth. Francis's great love flowed from his belief in the goodness of all creation. Francis knew God who is the Father-Creator, Son-Savior, and Holy Spirit-Sanctifier, and he knew that he was to be brother to all of creation. Francis was so totally rooted in the utter and supreme goodness of God that he could not help but love with all his being all that God had created. **We should recall the gentleness with which saints like St. Francis of Assisi or St. Philip Neri treated animals (2416).**

Zacchaeus climbed a sycamore tree to see what Jesus was like. In the process of meeting Jesus, he gained new insights. As you listen to his story, what new insights are yours?

Scripture: Pondering the Word   Luke 19:1-10

Sharing Question

- If I have ever taken what is not mine, what can I do about that now? Zacchaeus looked at his business dealings and responded to any injustice he may have incurred. In what ways have I been a good steward of what God has given to me (wealth, property, money, time, talents, etc.)?

Exploring the *Catechism* (continued)

Jesus showed compassion toward those who had followed him. From a totally inadequate supply of bread and fish, he provided for all who had hungered for his spiritual message (Mark 8:1-9). As a community of faith,

WHAT GOOD IS IT TO PROFESS FAITH WITHOUT PRACTICING IT

JAMES 2.14

we too are called to share "the work of our hands" and thus, to feed one another. When we work, we are present to God's call.

We can participate in the creative power of God by uniting our work to Christ. Whether we are employed or not, seeking employment, or working at our daily tasks, when we unite our work to Christ, we are participating in God's creative activity.

Our *Catechism* offers some clear directives on work. Any **system that "subordinates the basic rights of individuals and of groups to the collective organization of production" is contrary to human dignity** (*Gaudium et spes* 65 § 2) **(2424).** Work is our duty as well as a great gift from our Creator. In work, we both exercise and fulfill our potential. It is the right of every person to be able to draw from work the means of providing for the necessities of life as well as a means of serving the human community. **Work can be a means of sanctification and a way of animating earthly realities with the Spirit of Christ (2427-2428).**

When conflicts arise between employers and employees, efforts should be made to reduce these conflicts by a process of negotiation that respects the rights and duties of each entity **(2430). Those** *responsible for business enterprises* **are responsible to society for the economic and ecological effects of their operations. They have an obligation to consider the good of persons and not only the increase of** *profits* **(2432).**

All people are entitled to have *access to employment* and to professions **without unjust discrimination: men and women, healthy and disabled, natives and immigrants (2433)** should receive their just wages **(2434).** Perhaps one of the most difficult situations for a person to be in is to be unemployed or underemployed. ***Unemployment* almost always wounds its victim's dignity… (2436).**

Sharing Our Faith

- How do I see my work (whether paid or unpaid) as a means of sanctification?
- How might I better animate my part of society with the spirit of Christ?

Exploring the *Catechism* (continued)

While individual poverty is addressed by the Church so are the poverty and the inequality of resources of entire nations. Our *Catechism* instructs us that we are an international community, yet a community with many problems. **On the international level, inequality of resources and economic capability is such that it creates a real "gap" between nations. On the one side there are those nations possessing and developing the means of growth and, on the other, those accumulating debts (2437).**

We are called as a human community to **solidarity among nations which are already politically interdependent (2438).** *Rich nations* **have a grave moral responsibility toward those which are unable to ensure the**

in the wilderness JUSTICE will come to live ... I will send PEACE like a flowing river

means of their development by themselves or have been prevented from doing so by tragic historical events. It is a duty in solidarity and charity; it is also an obligation in justice if the prosperity of the rich nations has come from resources that have not been paid for fairly (2439). In addition, [t]he efforts of poor countries working for growth and liberation must be supported (2440).

There is no concept so key to Christianity as that of the value of the human person. A healthy self-esteem is based on our faith in God's unconditional love for each and every person. Human rights are God given. We need to help people help themselves. It is the task of countries with more to assist those with less, always focusing on making them self-sufficient. We are reminded that no country is to "lord it over" another (Matthew 20:25). Each country is morally bound to be in right relationship with other countries and to reach out to those who are struggling.

God blesses those who come to the aid of the poor and rebukes those who turn away from them... (2443). Jesus challenges us with a clear mandate as he talks about the Last Judgment (see Matthew 25:31-46). To abandon the poor is to abandon God. The Church has always taught a preferential option for the poor. **This love is inspired by the Gospel of the Beatitudes, of the poverty of Jesus, and of his concern for the poor. Love for the poor is even one of the motives for the duty of working so as to "be able to give to those in need"** (Ephesians 4:28). **It extends not only to material poverty but also to the many forms of cultural and religious poverty (2444).**

The Scriptures are filled with a preference for the poor. Luke 3:11 reminds us that anyone who has two coats must share with those who have none; and those with food must do likewise. James 2:15-16 tells us how to respond to the poor: "If a brother or sister is naked and lacks daily food, and one of you says to them, 'Go in peace; be warm and eat your fill,' and yet you do not supply their bodily needs, what is the good of that?" **(2447).**

As Church, we are called to address the problems of human misery. **When her mother reproached her for caring for the poor and the sick at** home, St. Rose of Lima said to her: "When we serve the poor and the sick, we serve Jesus. We must not fail to help our neighbors, because in them we serve Jesus" (2449).

Sharing Our Faith

- Jesus always spoke with conviction of those who were poor and the need to love the poor. Who are some of the poor and how do I respond to the challenge of this gospel?
- What, if any, experience have I had of being poor? How does this experience color my attitude to those who are considered poor today?
- If I am an employer, how do I treat my employees? With dignity and respect? Or as a means of profit? If I am an employee, do I give an honest day's work? Share about your work ethic.
- What could I do to assist developing countries and help with global economic balance? What steps can I take personally? What steps can we take as a group?

Living the Good News

Determine a specific action (individual or group) that flows from your sharing. This should be your primary consideration.

When choosing an individual action, determine what you will do and share it with the group. When choosing a group action, determine who will take responsibility for different aspects of the action.

The following are secondary suggestions:

- Make a commitment to improve your work relationship with your employer or employees.
- Think about Zacchaeus's response to Jesus. He gave half of his belongings to the poor. Give something that is very precious to you to a poor person or to an association that helps those who are truly poor.
- Take a walk and thank God for the beauty of creation. Join a group that takes responsibility for safeguarding our natural resources, for example, water, air, soil, forests.
- Create a "miracle of sharing" by offering your gifts to someone in need.
- Become familiar with legislation that will help to feed the hungry. Contact your representatives and urge them to pass such legislation.

- Build a personal relationship with a person from another country who is poor.

As my response to the gospel of Jesus, this week I commit to _____

_____ .

Lifting Our Hearts

Invite one person to pray Psalm 67.

Then offer spontaneous prayers and conclude with the Our Father.

Looking Ahead

- Prepare for your next session by prayerfully reading and studying
  — **Session 12: Human Fulfillment in Christ**
  — Scripture: Luke 21:1-4 (the poor widow's contribution)
  — the summary of doctrinal statements presented by the *United States Catholic Catechism for Adults* for the tenth commandment, pages 455-456

- You may like to consult the relevant chapter from the *United States Catholic Catechism for Adults*
  — Chapter 31 "The Tenth Commandment: Embrace Poverty of Spirit" from the *United States Catholic Catechism for Adults*

- You may also like to consult the relevant paragraphs from the *Catechism of the Catholic Church*:
  — paragraphs 2534-2557 on the tenth commandment

- Remember to use RENEWING FAMILY FAITH (see pages 82-83) and its helpful suggestions on how to extend the fruits of your sharing beyond your group, especially to your families.

Session 12
Human Fulfillment in Christ

†††

Suggested environment

Bible, candle, and, if possible, the *Catechism of the Catholic Church*
Begin with a quiet, reflective atmosphere.

Lifting Our Hearts

Song

"Every Tear That We Cry," Mark LeVang, *RENEW the Face of the Earth*,
Seasons 3 and 4

Pray together

Father in heaven,
you call us by name and invite us to friendship
with Jesus, your Son, by the power of the Holy Spirit.
Help us to overcome our selfishness.
Expand our hearts so that we become true followers
of him who lived for others rather than for himself.
Teach us to believe in your goodness,
to hope for your mercy, and to love our neighbors by freely sharing with
them the good news and mercy you have given us. Amen.

Sharing Our Good News

Share how you did with your **Living the Good News** *from the previous session.*

Exploring the *Catechism*

The tenth commandment: You shall not covet your neighbor's goods.

Matthew's Gospel tells us, "For where your treasure is, there your
heart will be also" (Matthew 6:21). The tenth commandment is about the
intentions of the heart.

**The sensitive appetite leads us to desire pleasant things we do not
have, e.g., the desire to eat when we are hungry or to warm ourselves**

when we are cold. These desires are good in themselves; but often they exceed the limits of reason and drive us to covet unjustly what is not ours and belongs to another or is owed to [that person] (2535).

The tenth commandment forbids greed, avarice, and envy, which are vices that bring about so much unhappiness in our world (2536–2540). Furthermore, these sins contribute to the frustration, anger, and depression that war against the divine charity that is poured into our hearts by the Holy Spirit.

Our discipleship with Jesus is a response to the call given to us by the Father. Like Jesus, we are to be led by the Spirit and follow the desires of the Spirit (Galatians 5:24-25). Our restless hearts can find fulfillment only by doing the will of God. It is not by fulfilling our sensitive appetite or by amassing great possessions, or even by achieving high positions that we fulfill our Father's will.

Jesus enjoins his disciples to prefer him to everything and everyone, and bids them "renounce all that [they have]" for his sake and that of the Gospel (2544).

SHE PUT IN EVERY-THING

ALL SHE HAD TO LIVE ON

Jesus taught his disciples detachment from earthly riches by telling many stories and pointing out examples. In Luke's Gospel, he gives us the example of a poor widow who put in the Temple treasury all she had to live on. This was her way of expressing total dependence upon God.

Scripture: Pondering the Word
Luke 21:1-4

Sharing Question

• In the gospel, the rich put in their "extra," the widow put in everything she had. In what areas do I feel called to give more than my "extra"?

Exploring the *Catechism* (continued)

Jesus blessed the poor widow. Jesus blessed those whose hearts were emptied of arrogance and false pride. So, too, he blesses us when we trust him, when we empty ourselves of arrogance, false pride, and all that holds us back from him. He asks us to be grateful for the gifts we have received and to be humble in the face of God's goodness and generosity (2545-2546).

Abandonment to the providence of the Father in heaven frees us from anxiety about tomorrow. Trust in God is a preparation for the blessedness of the poor. They shall see God (2547).

The culture of our times encourages us to acquire possessions, pleasure, power, and popularity, but if our happiness depends solely on these factors, we shall never achieve peace of heart. True happiness and lasting fulfillment require us to love one another as Jesus loves us. This means we are empowered by his Spirit to deny our immoderate cravings and overcome our envy of others. We learn to bless people from our hearts and to praise God for the spiritual and material gifts they have received. We struggle to accept our losses and deprivations, but we know that our treasure is not in this world where we have "no abiding city." St. Paul reminds us: "If for this life only we have hoped in Christ, we are of all people most to be pitied" (1 Corinthians 15:19).

When Jesus tells us there are many mansions in his Father's house (John 14:2), he is reminding us that our true dwelling place is not in this world. He wants us to realize that, in this life, like the grain of wheat, we must die to ourselves. We must **mortify** [our] **cravings and, with the grace of God, prevail over the seductions of pleasure and power (2549)** and enter into the peace of the Lord. God calls us to perfect joy (Revelation 22:17). We who follow Jesus can find no greater satisfaction than in the faith, hope, and love he has given us and in the promise of seeing God.

"Who will separate us from the love of Jesus Christ?" (Romans 8:35).

KEEP AWAKE FOR YOU DO NOT KNOW ON WHAT DAY YOUR LORD IS COMING. MATTHEW 24.42

Under the influence of grace, we learn to keep the commandments and to live the Beatitudes. By the power of the Holy Spirit, we leave behind our false pride, our lust, our selfishness, our envy, and all the sin that wounded us in the past. We learn to love others as we ourselves are loved. Now, at last, we are ready to share even in this world, the life of the saints in heaven with God **(2557).**

Sharing Our Faith

- What treasure is hidden most deep in my heart?

- Read Romans 8:35. What feelings rise in my heart when I read this passage?
- What do I most love about Jesus Christ? How can I share this message with others?

Living the Good News

Determine a specific action (individual or group) that flows from your sharing. This should be your primary consideration.

When choosing an individual action, determine what you will do and share it with the group. When choosing a group action, determine who will take responsibility for different aspects of the action.

The following are secondary suggestions:

- Continue to meet as a small community using one of the three other books in this *Why Catholic? Journey through the Catechism* Series:
    The Profession of Faith: What We Believe
    The Celebration of the Christian Mystery: Sacraments
    Christian Prayer: Deepening My Experience of God.
- Share some aspect of the treasure of your faith with another person this week.
- Reach out in generosity to someone (or to a group) who has suffered a loss or is deprived of the basic essentials of life. Share something meaningful to you with that person (or group).
- Write a letter to the editor of your diocesan paper or a local newspaper regarding an aspect of your faith.
- Spend some time in prayer, giving your heart over to God.
- Decide as a group to continue to meet and support one another on your faith journey. See **Looking Ahead** below.
- Celebrate in a special way with your group through a prayer or social event.

As my response to the gospel of Jesus, this week I commit to _____

_____ .

Lifting Our Hearts

Invite one person to proclaim Matthew 6:19-34. Reflect quietly. Then share a word, a phrase, or a line that had meaning for you.

Offer spontaneous prayers, and then pray together the Our Father.

Exchange the sign of peace with each other.

Looking Ahead

- Over 50 other faith-sharing titles are available through

   RENEW International
   1232 George Street
   Plainfield, NJ 07062-1717
   Phone   908-769-5400
   To order   888-433-3221
   Fax   908-769-5660
   Web sites   www.renewintl.org
                  www.WhyCatholic.org
   E-mail   Resources@renewintl.org

Music Resources

OCP

For CDs, printed music, downloadable mp3 files (via iTunes) contact:
Oregon Catholic Press Publications
5536 NE Hassalo
Portland, OR 97213

Phone	800-LITURGY (548-8749)
Fax	800-4-OCP-FAX (462-7329)
Website	www.ocp.org
E-mail	liturgy@ocp.org

For permission to reprint words and/or music, contact:
         www.licensingonline.org

RENEW

For cassettes of the RENEW the Face of the Earth *albums, contact:*
RENEW International
1232 George Street
Plainfield, NJ 07062-1717

To order	888-433-3221
Fax	908-769-5660
Website	www.renewintl.org

White Dove

For CDs and song books of the RENEW the Face of the Earth *albums, contact:*
White Dove Productions, Inc.

Phone	520-219-3824
Website	www.whitedoveproductions.com
E-mail	info@whitedoveproductions.com

Further Reading

Pope John XXIII. Encyclical Letter, *Pacem in Terris (Peace on Earth)*. Washington, DC: United States Conference of Catholic Bishops, 1963, revised edition 2003.

United States Conference of Catholic Bishops. A Pastoral Letter, *A Place at the Table: A Catholic Recommitment to Overcome Poverty and to Respect the Dignity of All God's Children*. Washington, DC: United States Conference of Catholic Bishops, 2002.

_____. Tenth Anniversary Edition of *Economic Justice for All: Pastoral Letter on Catholic Social Teaching and the U.S. Economy*. Washington, DC: United States Conference of Catholic Bishops, 1997.

_____. *Human Sexuality: A Catholic Perspective for Education and Lifelong Learning*. Washington, DC: United States Conference of Catholic Bishops, 1991.

_____. A Pastoral Letter Concerning Migration from the Catholic Bishops of Mexico and the United States, *Strangers No Longer: Together on the Journey of Hope*. Washington, DC: United States Conference of Catholic Bishops, 2003.

_____. A Pastoral Letter, *The Challenge of Peace: God's Promise and Our Response*. Washington, DC: United States Conference of Catholic Bishops, 2000.

Education for Justice Project. Center of Concern, 1225 Otis Street NE, Washington, DC, 20017. Phone: 202-635-2757 x131, Web site: http://www.educationforjustice.org, E-mail: efj@coc.org

Why Catholic? Resources from RENEW

RENEWING FAMILY FAITH:
We Believe, We Celebrate, We Live, We Pray

RENEWING FAMILY FAITH is a resource designed to extend the experience of the *Why Catholic?* process so that the faith sharing it promotes can become an integral part of whole family catechesis.

For every Session offered by the *Why Catholic?* faith-sharing books there is a corresponding practical, informative two-page bulletin in full color: a total of 48 in all (12 for each of the four *Why Catholic?* faith-sharing books).

These Bulletins have been produced to facilitate sharing within the family on exactly the same themes the adults are exploring together in their *Why Catholic?* faith-sharing sessions.

Each issue offers:

- an interesting selection of faith reflections for parents
- a wide variety of family activities
- questions that encourage table sharing
- brief scripture passages and wisdom quotes
- an inspiring story on the life of an honored saint or a modern person who has lived an extraordinary faith life

This is a resource which can serve in a variety of creative ways: to reach and assist those whom for some reason are unable to take part in the Sunday celebration of Mass: those who are the sick or homebound.

It can also be used in sacramental preparation programs, and for homily preparation.

Here is the content for each Bulletin, designed to correspond and complement the Sessions in this *Life in Christ* faith-sharing book:

1. **Living Beatitudes**
   Our Story: American Author
      (Flannery O'Connor)
   Parenting: Reading
   Family Activities: Doing Beatitudes
   Pondering the Word: Matthew 5:9
   CCC: 1708

2. **Religious Freedom**
   Our Story: John Courtney
      Murray, S.J.
   Parenting: Expressing Faith
   Family Activities: Learning the Way
   Pondering the Word: John 13:34
   CCC: 1745

3. **Forming Conscience**
   Our Story: St. Thomas Aquinas:
      A Great Thinker
   Parenting: Conscience
   Family Activities: Signs of
      the Time
   Pondering the Word: Romans 2:15
   CCC: 1788

5. **Samaritan Woman**
   Our Story: Martin de Porres
   Parenting: Spirituality of
      Parenting
   Family Activities: Sharing Values
   Pondering the Word: John 4:24
   CCC: 1888

7. **Loving God**
   Our Story: St. Augustine
   Parenting: Sharing Feelings
   Family Activities: Family Home
      Blessing
   Pondering the Word: Matthew 19:16
   CCC: 2158

9. **Faith Builds on Life**
   Our Story: Teresa of Avila
   Parenting: Talking with Children
   Family Activities: Quality of Life
   Pondering the Word: Matthew 5:24
   CCC: 2270

11. **Two Paths**
   Our Story: St. Thomas More
   Parenting: Common Good
   Family Activities: Doing Good
   Pondering the Word: Luke 19:10
   CCC: 2427-2428

4. **Virtues**
   Our Story: Rose of Lima
   Parenting: Having or Being?
   Family Activities: Conversion:
      Growth and Change
   Pondering the Word: John 15:9-10
   CCC: 1811

6. **Natural Law**
   Our Story: Frances Xavier Cabrini
   Parenting: Your Holy Imagination
   Family Activities: Remembrance
   Pondering the Word: Colossians 1:3
   CCC: 1701

8. **Jesus As a Teen**
   Our Story: Growing in Trust
      (St. Marguerite)
   Parenting: Affirming Language
   Family Activities: Family Meaning
   Pondering the Word: Luke 2:48
   CCC: 2224

10. **Love and Marriage**
   Our Story: Pierre Toussaint
   Parenting: Spirituality at Work
   Family Activities: Sharing Grace
   Pondering the Word: John 15:12
   CCC: 2348-2349

12. **Spirituality of Work**
   Our Story: A Great Monk
      (St. Benedict of Nursia)
   Parenting: Workplace
   Family Activities: Homework
   Pondering the Word: Luke 21:3
   CCC: 2544

Notes